AUTOMATED WEB SCRAPING

FROM BASICS

TO

ADVANCED TECHNIQUES

BY

Christie M. Brown

Table of Contents

Chapter 1 8

What is web scraping? 8

Chapter 2 12

The Importance and Applications of Web Scraping..............12

Chapter 3 17

Ethical Considerations for Web Scraping.....................17

Chapter 4 21

Understanding The Structure of Web Pages......................21

Chapter 5 27

Introduction to HTML Tags. 27

Chapter 6 32

Understanding HTML attributes 32

Chapter 7 39

Popular Web Scraping Libraries and Frameworks 39

Chapter 8 48

Browser Developer Tools for Inspection......................48

Chapter 9 58

When should you use APIs vs web scraping? 58

Chapter 10 65

Legal Aspects of Web Scraping 65

Chapter 11 71

Best Practices to Minimize Legal Risk 71

Chapter 12 75

Implement ethical scraping practices: 75

Chapter 13 79

    Best practices for ethical scraping 79

Chapter 14 88

    Installation and Configuration for Web Scraping................. 88

Chapter 15 96

    Navigating HTML Documents 96

Chapter 16 104

    Extracting Data with BeautifulSoup 104

Chapter 17 112

    Handling JavaScript-generated Content 112

Chapter 18 120

    Advanced Methods for Dynamic Content Extraction 120

Chapter 19 130

    Parsing the extracted data... 130

Chapter 20 139

    Handling JavaScript-generated Content 139

Chapter 21 146

    Advanced Methods for Dynamic Content Extraction 147

Chapter 22 158

    Parsing the extracted data... 158

Chapter 23 168

    Handling Errors and Exceptions during Web Scraping........ 168

Chapter 24 178

    Cleaning and preparing scraped data. 178

Chapter 25 196

    Cleaning and preparing scraped data. 196

Chapter 26 212

    User Agent Rotation 212

Chapter 27 215

    Parallel scraping techniques 215

Chapter 28 220

    Load balancing and scaling 220

Chapter 29 225

    Optimization Tips for Efficient Scraping..............225

Chapter 30 230

    Scraping data from e-commerce sites 230

Chapter 31 235

    Extracting Data from Social Media Platforms......235

Chapter 32 241

    Real-world examples and challenges...................241

Chapter 33 244

    Conclusion 244

Chapter 1

What is web scraping?

Web scraping is the automated extraction of data from websites. It entails accessing web pages using software or scripts, retrieving HTML material, and parsing that text to extract the desired information. This approach enables users to collect enormous volumes of data rapidly and effectively, which may then be utilized for a variety of reasons, including analysis, research, and integration into other systems.

Key Features of Web Scraping

Fetching the Web Page: The first step is to submit an HTTP request to a web server to retrieve the HTML content of a web page. This may be accomplished using a variety of frameworks and techniques, such as requests in Python.

Parsing the HTML: Once the HTML material has been obtained, it must be processed to extract relevant data. This is commonly accomplished with parsing packages such as BeautifulSoup or XML.

Data extraction is the process of identifying and extracting certain data points after processing HTML. This may entail identifying HTML elements, attributes, and values that provide the needed information.

The extracted data is then saved in a structured format, such as CSV, JSON, or a database, for further study or usage.

Example Workflow

Identify the target website. Select the website and the individual pages from which you wish to scrape data.

Inspect the page structure. Use browser developer tools to examine the HTML structure of web pages and find the tags and attributes containing the needed data.

Write a Scraper Script: Using a programming language like Python and tools such as BeautifulSoup or Scrapy, create a script that automates the fetching, parsing, and extraction processes.

Run the script. Run the script to scrape data from the webpage.

Process and store data: Clean, analyze, and save scraped data in a usable format.

Applications for Web Scraping

Market research involves gathering pricing and product information from e-commerce websites.

Data aggregation is the process of compiling data from many sources to produce comprehensive databases.

Sentiment Analysis: Gathering user feedback and social media posts for sentiment analysis.

News monitoring is tracking news stories and updates from various news websites.

The academic study includes extracting data from publicly available websites.

Web scraping is a versatile and effective technology for automating web data collecting, making enormous datasets easier to obtain and analyze. However, it is critical to address the ethical and legal elements of online scraping in order to ensure compliance with applicable rules and respect for website owners' rights.

Chapter 2

The Importance and Applications of Web Scraping

Web scraping automates data collecting, saving time and effort over human entry. This is especially useful for dealing with enormous datasets or constantly altering information.

Access to Real-Time Data: It provides access to current information, which is critical in businesses that rely on real-time data, such as banking, e-commerce, and journalism.

Web scraping improves data analysis by obtaining data from several sources, allowing for more thorough analysis and insights that can drive company plans, academic research, and market trends.

Competitive Advantage: Companies may maintain their competitiveness by monitoring rivals' prices, goods, and consumer feedback. This allows them to alter their strategy to match market needs.

Cost-effective: Using web scraping to automate data collecting reduces the requirement for manual labor while also speeding up the data acquisition process.

Applications of Web Scraping include market research and competitor analysis.

Pricing Intelligence is the process of collecting pricing data from competing websites in order to assess trends and determine competitive rates.

Product comparisons involve gathering product information and reviews to compare features and quality.

Data Aggregation and Integration:

Real Estate Listings: Compiling property listings from many real estate websites into a comprehensive database.

Job postings: Bringing together job openings from numerous job boards to create a single job search platform.

Academic and scientific research:

Social science studies involve gathering social media data, public documents, and other internet resources for sociological and psychological research.

Environmental Monitoring: Extracting information from weather websites, government databases, and scientific publications for environmental study.

Sentiment Analysis and Social Media Monitoring:

Customer feedback is the extraction of customer reviews from e-commerce sites in order to assess sentiment and enhance products or services.

Brand monitoring involves scraping social media sites and forums to track public opinion and brand reputation.

Financial Analysis and Stock Market Monitoring:

Stock Prices: Collecting real-time stock prices and financial news for research and trading.

Economic indicators are data extracted from government and financial institution websites in order to anticipate economic conditions.

Content Aggregation and News Monitoring:

News Feeds: Articles gathered from several news sources to give a consolidated news service.

Event tracking involves monitoring events and updates from many sources to keep people updated.

E-commerce and online retailing:

Inventory management involves scraping supplier websites to keep track of stock levels and product availability.

Product Listings: Automated extraction of product information and photos for online shop catalogs.

Travel & Tourism:

Flight and Hotel Aggregation: Gathering flight schedules, pricing, and hotel availability from several travel websites to offer a full booking solution.

Scraping travel blogs and tourist websites to get location guides and reviews.

Web scraping is a flexible technique that may be used across sectors to automate data collecting, obtain competitive insights, and aid decision-making processes. However, online scraping must be done in an ethical and legal manner, in accordance with website terms of service and data protection rules.

Chapter 3

Ethical Considerations for Web Scraping

Web scraping, while powerful and beneficial, needs careful consideration of ethical norms to guarantee that use is both responsible and lawful. Here are some important ethical concerns to keep in mind:

1. Following the Terms of Service

Read and follow the Terms of Service: Many websites include terms of service that specify if and how their data may be accessed and used. Scraping websites that specifically ban scraping may result in legal penalties.

Compliance: Always adhere to the website's terms and conditions to avoid illegal data access and associated legal consequences.

2. Avoiding Overload. Servers

Rate limitation: Use rate limitation in your scraping scripts to avoid sending too many requests in a short time. This helps to avoid overwhelming the website's server, which might impair service for other users.

Polite Scraping: Use tactics such as setting proper time intervals between queries and tracking the impact of your scraping activity on the website's performance.

3. Ensuring privacy and data security

Personal Data: Exercise caution while scraping personal information, particularly if it is not expressly public. Collecting personal data without authorization may breach privacy rules such as the GDPR (General Data Protection Regulation) or the CCPA (California Consumer Privacy Act).

Data Anonymization: If personal information is obtained, it should be anonymized or handled in a way that protects individuals' privacy.

4. Transparency and Attribution: When using scraped data for public or commercial reasons, cite the original sources appropriately. This

appreciates the content providers' efforts while also respecting intellectual property rights.

Transparency: Be open and honest about your data-gathering processes, especially if you want to use the data publicly or commercially.

5. Compliance with Legal Regulations

Legal Advice: Consult a lawyer to learn about the legal ramifications of web scraping in your jurisdiction. distinct nations have distinct regulations governing data access and scraping.

Copyright & Intellectual Property: Respect the copyright laws and intellectual property rights. Scraping copyrighted information without authorization might result in legal issues.

6. Ethical Data Use: Ensure that scraped data is used responsibly. Avoid utilizing scraped data for nefarious goals like spamming, disseminating disinformation, or invading people's privacy.

Fair usage: Consider if the data usage is consistent with fair use standards, such as educational purposes, research, or commentary.

7. Technical measures to prevent abuse.

IP Blocking and Bans: Be aware that websites can identify and prevent scraping activity. Techniques such as proxy rotation and user-agent rotation should be used responsibly, not to avoid legal blocking mechanisms.

Respect robots.txt: Many websites utilize the robots.txt file to convey their scraping policy. While not legally obligatory, following robots.txt instructions is regarded as best practice in ethical site scraping.

8. Data Contribution: Share insights, make changes, or collaborate on data-sharing agreements with the community or website you're scraping from.

By following these ethical principles, you may guarantee that your online scraping operations are carried out ethically, respecting the rights of website owners and users, and in accordance with applicable laws and regulations.

Chapter 4

Understanding The Structure of Web Pages

To efficiently scrape data from websites, you must first grasp the structure of the web pages. Web pages are mostly made up of HTML (Hypertext Markup Language), which specifies the content and structure, and CSS (Cascading Style Sheets), which determines the presentation. Here's an outline of the main components and concepts:

1. HTML Basics

HTML is a markup language used to define the structure of online pages. It is made up of a sequence of pieces that are separated by tags. Tags are frequently seen in pairs: an opening tag and a closing tag.

Here's an example of an HTML document:
<!DOCTYPE html> <html> <head> <title>Sample Web Page.</title> </head> <body> <h1>Welcome to my website!</h1>

```html
<p>This is a piece of text from my webpage.</p>                    <a href="https://www.example.com">Visit Example.<a> </body> </html>.
```

2. Common HTML Elements.

<html> is the root element of an HTML document.

<head>: It includes meta-information about the document, such as the title and links to stylesheets.

<title>: Determines the title of the web page (seen in the browser tab).

The <body> tag contains the web page's content.

<h1>, <h2>, <h3>, and more. Header tags are used to define headers. <h1> is the highest-level heading.

<p>: The paragraph element is used to define a block of content.

<a>: An anchor tag is used to create hyperlinks.

<div>: The division tag is used to organize and group material.

<span> is a container for text and other inline elements.

3. HTML Attributions

Attributes include extra information about HTML components. They are included in the opening tag.

The id attribute uniquely identifies an element.

class: Defines one or more class names for an element, which are used for CSS styling.

The href attribute specifies the URL of a link (used in <a> tags).

The <img> element uses the src attribute to provide the image's source.

Example using attributes in HTML.

<p id="intro" class="text">.This is a paragraph containing id and class attributes.</p> <a

href="https://www.example.com"
class="link">.Visit Example</a>

4. CSS Basics.

CSS styles HTML components and controls their layout.

CSS Example:

```
/* External CSS file */ body { background-color: #f0f0f0; font-family: Arial, sans-serif; }
```

```
h1 { color: #333; }
```

```
.text { font-size: 16px;
```

```
.link { color: blue; text-decoration: none; }.
```

Inline CSS Example: HTML

```
<p      style="color:red;      font-size:14px;">This
paragraph contains inline CSS.</p>
```

5. Using Browser Developer Tools.

Web scraping requires the use of developer tools, which are included in modern web browsers.

These tools let you investigate HTML structure, view CSS styles, and troubleshoot JavaScript.

Right-click on a web page element and select "Inspect" to view its HTML and CSS.

Elements Panel: View and browse the document object model (DOM) tree.

Network Panel: Monitor network requests to better understand how data is loaded on a website.

To interact with the web page and diagnose bugs, use the Console Panel to run JavaScript code.

6. Understanding the Document Object Model (DOM).

The DOM is the programming interface for HTML pages. It represents the page, allowing applications to modify the document's structure, design, and content. The DOM is a tree-like structure, with each node representing an HTML element.

Here's an example of a simple DOM structure in HTML: <!DOCTYPE html> <html> <head> <title>Page Title: </title> </head> <body> <h1>Heading:</h1> <p>Paragraph </body> </html>

This HTML document's DOM structure is as follows:

bash html ├── head | ├── title | └── "Page Title" ├── body ├── h1 | └── "Heading ├── p └── "Paragraph"

Understanding the structure of online pages, HTML elements, attributes, and the function of CSS will allow you to efficiently discover and extract the data you want utilizing web scraping techniques.

Chapter 5

Introduction to HTML Tags.

HTML is the standard language for building web pages. HTML tags are the fundamental components of HTML that define elements and their properties inside a page. Here's an overview of several basic HTML tags and their uses.

Basic HTML Document Structure

HTML documents are arranged hierarchically, beginning with the <!DOCTYPE html> declaration and continue with the <html>, <head>, and <body> elements.

Here's an example of a basic HTML document: <!DOCTYPE html> <html> <head> <title>My web page </title> </head> <body> <h1>Welcome to my webpage.</h1> <p>This is one paragraph of text.<p> </body> </html>.

Common HTML Tags and Their Usage <!DOCTYPE HTML>

Purpose: Declares the HTML document type and version.

Example: <!DOCTYPE html> <html>

The purpose of the root element is to contain all other HTML components.

Attributes: lang (specifies the language of the document).

Example: <html lang="en"> <head>

Purpose: Provides meta-information about the document, such as the title and connections to CSS stylesheets and scripts.

Example: html.

<head> <title>My Web Page </title> <link rel="stylesheet" href="styles.css">

</head> <title>

Sets the web page's title, which is shown in the browser tab.

Example: <title>My Web Page</title> <body>

Purpose: Contains the web page's content, including text, graphics, and other features.

Example: HTML: <body> <h1>Welcome to my webpage.</h1> <p>This is one paragraph of text.</p> </body> <h1>, <h2>, <h3>, and more.

Purpose: Define headers for different levels. <h1> is the top level, followed by <h2>, <h3>, and so on.

Example: html.

<h1>Main Heading </h1> <h2>Subheading:</h2> <h3>Subheading</h3> <p>

Purpose: Defines a paragraph of text.

Example: <p>This is one paragraph.</p> <a>

Purpose: Defines a hyperlink, which connects to another website or resource.

Attributes include href (the URL of the link).

Example URL: <a href="https://www.example.com">Visit Example</a> <image>

The purpose is to embed a picture on the web page.

Attributes include the image's URL (src) and alternative text (alt).

Example: <img src="image.jpg" alt="Description of image">

~ul>, <ol>, <li>

The purpose is to define lists. The <ul> tag generates an unordered list, <ol> makes an ordered list, and <li> specifies a list item.

Example: html.

<ul> <li>Item 1: <li>Item 2:</li> </ul> <ol> <li>First item </li>Second item:</li> </ol> <div>

The purpose of defining a division or section in an HTML page is to arrange block-level material together.

Example: <div class="container">This is where the content goes.

Purpose: Defines an inline piece of text for grouping inline items.

Example: <span class="highlight">Highlighted text</span> <form>, <input>, and <button>

Create a form to collect user input. The form is defined by <form>, the input field by <input>, and the clickable button by <button> tags.

Attributes include action, method (for forms), type, name, and value (for inputs).

For example, with HTML: <form action="/submit" method="post"> <input type="text" name="username">.

  <button type="Submit">Submit (button) </form>

Chapter 6

Understanding HTML attributes

Attributes include extra information about HTML components. They are always included in the starting tag of an element.

Common Attributes:

id: Provides a unique identification for an element.

Example: <p id="intro">This is an introductory paragraph.</p>

class: Assigns one or more class names to an element for use in CSS style.

Example: <p class="text">This is a stylized paragraph.</p>

style: Adds inline CSS styles to an element.

Example: <p style="color: blue;">This paragraph is blue.</p>

Understanding HTML elements and properties is essential for web construction and scraping. It helps you to detect and extract certain data items from web pages quickly.

Overview of CSS Selectors.

CSS (Cascading Style Sheets) is used to design and layout web pages. CSS selectors are patterns used to choose which elements to style. Understanding CSS selectors is essential for applying styles properly and online scraping, as selectors are frequently used to discover parts within HTML pages.

Types of CSS Selectors

Basic selectors.

Universal Selector (*): selects all items.

Example: * {color: blue;}

Type Selector (Element Selector): Selects all items of a specified type.

Example: p { font-size: 16px; }.

Class Selector

Selects all items with the specified class property. Classes are denoted by a dot (.) before the class name.

Example:.highlight { background-color: yellow; }.

Use in HTML: <p class="Highlight">This text is highlighted.</p>

ID Selector

Selects a single element with the provided id attribute. IDs are defined with a hash (#) preceding the id name.

Example: #main { width: 100%; }.

Use in HTML: <div id="main">.Main Content</div>

Attribute Selector

Chooses items depending on the presence or value of an attribute.

Example: a[href]. {color: red;} (Selects all <a> components with href attribute)

Example: input[type="text"]. {border:1px solid #000;} (Selects all text entry fields)

Pseudo classes and pseudo-elements

Pseudo-classes: Choose items according to their state.

Example: a:hover {color: green;} (Changes link color when hovered)

Pseudo-elements: Choose and style components of an element.

Example: p::first-line. {Font-weight: bold;} (Styles the first line of each paragraph.)

Example: p::before. { text: "Note: "; color: red; } (Adds material before every paragraph)

Combinator selectors

Descendant Selector (Space): Finds all elements that are descendants of a specific element.

Example: div p { color: blue; }. (This selects all <p> elements within <div> elements.)

The Child Selector (>) selects items that are direct children of a given element.

Example: ul > li { list-style-type: none; }. (This selects all <li> components that are direct children of <ul>.)

Adjacent Sibling Selector (+): Selects the element that is the next sibling of a given element.

Example: h1 + p { margin-top: 0; }. (Selects the <p> element just after a <h1>)

The General Sibling Selector (~) selects all items that are siblings of the given element.

Example: h1 ~ p { color: gray; }. (Chooses all <p> elements that are siblings of a <h1>.)

Specificity and Inheritance

Specificity: Specifies which CSS rule is used when multiple rules match the same element. Specificity is calculated using the types of selectors employed.

Inline styles (style attributes): Highest specificity

ID Selectors: High specificity.

Selectors for classes, attributes, and pseudo-classes: Moderate specificity.

Type selectors and pseudo-elements: Low specificity.

Universal selector: lowest specificity.

Inheritance: CSS characteristics like color and font family are passed down from parent elements to offspring.

Example of combining selectors

You can use numerous selections to apply more particular styles.

CSS: /* Selects all <a> elements inside a <nav> with the class "menu" */ nav.menu a. { text-decoration: none; color: white; }

/* This selects the <p> element with the id "intro" */ p#intro { font-size: 18px; font-weight: bold; }

Understanding and successfully using CSS selectors is critical for styling online pages and detecting items while scraping web data. This information is useful in developing accurate and efficient rules for both style and data extraction.

Chapter 7

Popular Web Scraping Libraries and Frameworks

Web scraping is the process of obtaining data from web pages, and various strong tools and frameworks have been built to help with this. Here are a few of the most popular:

1. Beautiful Soup.

BeautifulSoup is a Python package that parses HTML and XML texts. It generates a parse tree for parsed pages, which may be used to extract data from HTML, even if the HTML is not well structured.

Installation: pip install beautifulsoup4.

Usage: Frequently used with the requests library to get web pages.

Key features:

Simple to use and learn.

Accepts badly structured HTML gently.

Various parsers are supported, including XML, and HTML. parser, and html5lib.

Example:

Python: import requests from bs4 import BeautifulSoup

url = 'https://example.com', response = requests.get(url), soup = BeautifulSoup(response.content, 'html.parser').

```
# Extracting data.

Title = soup.title.string Links = soup.find_all('a')

Print("Title:", title) For the link in links:

    print("Link:", link.get('href').
```

2. Scrapy.

Scrapy is an open-source web crawling platform developed in Python. It is used to take data from websites, process it, and store it in an organized manner.

Installation: pip install scrapy.

Usage: Suitable for large-scale web scraping and web crawler development.

Key features:

Built-in capabilities for processing requests, navigating links, and extracting data.

Middleware support for handling requests and answers.

Ability to export data in a variety of formats, including JSON, CSV, and XML.

Example:

Create a scrappy project and a spider:

To start a project, use the following commands: bash, scrappy, cd, and get spider.

Editing example.py:

Python: import scrappy.

Class ExampleSpider (scrappy. Spider):

```
    Name:        'example'        Start        URLs:
['https://example.com']

    Define    parse(self,    response):    title    =
response.css('title::text').get()        links        =
response.css('a::attr(href)').getall()

        yield { 'title': title, 'links': links }
```

Run the spider:

```
Bash: scrapy crawl example -o output.json 3.
Selenium
```

Selenium is a browser automation tool that may be used to scrape online pages, particularly those that rely heavily on JavaScript to load content.

Installation: pip install selenium.

Controls a web browser using a driver (for example, ChromeDriver for Google Chrome).

Key features:

Supports dynamic content and JavaScript.

Can imitate user behaviors like clicks and form submissions.

Example:

Python originates from selenium. Import webdriver from Selenium.webdriver.common.by. By

```
# Configure the driver: driver = webdriver.Chrome(executable_path='/path/to/chromedriver') driver.get('https://example.com')
```

```
# Extracting data: title = driver.title links = driver.find_elements(By.TAG_NAME, 'a')
```

```
Print("Title:", title) For the link in links:
    print("Link:", link.get_attribute('href').
```

driver.quit()

4. Requests-HTML is a Python package that combines the convenience of requests with the capabilities of XML to parse HTML. It can render JavaScript, making it ideal for scraping dynamic material.

Installation: pip install requests-html.

Usage: Simple to use, with integrated JavaScript rendering capability.

Key features:

Simplifies the process of scraping JavaScript-rich webpages.

Offers a robust API for browsing and retrieving data from HTML.

Example:

Python: from requests_html import HTMLSession.

session = HTMLSession().

```
response  =  session.get('https://example.com');
response.html.render().
```

```
# Extracting data: title = response.html.find('title',
first=true).Text                Links                =
response.html.absolute_links
```

```
Print("Title:", title) For the link in links:

  Print("Link:", link)
```

5. lxml

Lxml is a sophisticated Python package for processing XML and HTML. It relies on the libxml2 and libxslt libraries.

Installation: pip install lxml.

Usage: It provides high-performance parsing and can handle huge documents effectively.

Key features are fast performance and memory efficiency.

Allows for complex queries and transformations using XPath and XSLT.

Example:

Python: import requests from lxml, then import html.

url = 'https://example.com', response = requests.get(url), and tree = html.fromstring(response.content).

Extracting data.

Title = tree.xpath('//title/text()').[0]

Links = tree.xpath('//a/@href').

Print("Title:", title) For the link in links:

   Print("Link:", link)

These libraries and frameworks offer a wide range of tools and features to meet a variety of online scraping requirements, from simple data extraction to extensive web crawling and dynamic content processing. Each has advantages, thus the choice of library is determined by the unique needs of the web scraping work at hand.

Chapter 8

Browser Developer Tools for Inspection.

Browser Developer Tools (DevTools) are a sophisticated set of features included in current web browsers. They provide a variety of functions that are extremely useful for web developers and web scrapers, allowing them to inspect and interact with online pages, diagnose bugs, and assess performance. Here's a full tutorial on how to use DevTools for site inspection and scraping:

Accessing the Developer Tools

To launch Developer Tools in most browsers:

In Google Chrome, right-click a webpage and select "Inspect," or use Ctrl+Shift+I (Windows/Linux) or Cmd+Opt+I (Mac).

Mozilla Firefox: Right-click a webpage and select "Inspect Element," or press Ctrl+Shift+I (Windows/Linux) or Cmd+Opt+I (Mac).

In Microsoft Edge, right-click a webpage and select "Inspect," or use Ctrl+Shift+I (Windows/Linux) or Cmd+Opt+I (Mac).

Key panels and their uses

Elements Panel

Inspect and edit the HTML and CSS of a webpage.

Features:

DOM Tree: Explore and browse the Document Object Model (DOM) tree, which represents the structure of an HTML document.

CSS Styles: View and modify CSS styles applied to specific components.

Visualize the box model (margin, border, padding, and content) of the elements.

The right-click Context Menu provides choices such as "Edit as HTML," "Copy," "Hide element," and so on.

Usage Example:

html

```
<body>
```

Welcome to my website, <h1 class="header">.

This is an example paragraph.

```
<a    href="https://example.com">Go    to
Example</a>
```

```
</body>
```

To investigate the <h1> tag, right-click and choose "Inspect."

The Elements panel will highlight the <h1 class="header">...</h1> element in the DOM tree and show its CSS style.

Console Panel

Purpose: Run JavaScript code and observe console messages (such as log outputs and faults).

Features:

JavaScript Execution: Execute JavaScript snippets from the current page.

Logging: Show messages from console.log, console.error, etc.

Error Reporting: See JavaScript errors and stack traces.

Usage Example:

javascript

```
Document.querySelectorAll('a').forEach(link => console.log(link.href));
```

The script reports all hyperlinks (<a> tags) on the current page to the console.

Network Panel

Monitor network requests and answers, which include HTML, CSS, JavaScript, pictures, and XHR queries.

Features:

Request Details: See full information about each request, including headers, payloads, and responses.

Performance Analysis: Examine load times and network performance.

Requests can be filtered based on their kind, status, domain, and other criteria.

Usage Example:

Load a page and select the Network tab to view all network activities.

Click on a request to see its information, such as headers, response data, and time.

Source Panel

Goal: Debug JavaScript code, see source files, and create breakpoints.

Features:

File System: Explore the site's file structure.

Set breakpoints, walk through code, and check variables.

Local Overrides: Change source files locally for testing.

Usage Example:

Set a breakpoint in a JavaScript file and reload the page to halt execution at the specified line.

Step through the code and analyze variable values using the debugging tools provided.

Application Panel

The purpose is to inspect and manage storage, cookies, and application data.

Features:

Local Storage: You may see and alter data from your local storage and session storage.

Cookies: Inspect and manage cookies placed by the website.

IndexedDB/Web SQL: View the site's databases.

Cache Management: Check service workers and cache storage.

Usage Example:

View and change the value of a particular key in Local Storage.

Performance Panel

Purpose: Evaluate the performance of your web application.

Features:

Recording: Save performance data for a specific session.

Analysis: Get a full breakdown of the page's performance, such as scripting, rendering, and painting.

Flame Chart: Visualize CPU activity over time.

Usage Example:

Record a performance session while loading a website and analyze the results to find bottlenecks.

Lighthouse Panel

Conduct audits to improve the quality of websites.

Features:

Audits: Evaluate performance, accessibility, SEO, and best practices.

Reports: Create thorough reports that include actionable suggestions.

Usage Example:

Conduct a Lighthouse audit and evaluate the results to detect and address performance and accessibility concerns.

Practical Applications for Web Scraping

Inspecting HTML Structure: Use the Elements tab to navigate the HTML structure and locate the tags, classes, and IDs associated with the data you wish to scrape.

Locating Selectors: Determine the best CSS selectors to utilize for extracting certain items.

Testing JavaScript: Use the Console panel to run JavaScript code snippets for data extraction and page interaction.

Monitoring Network Requests: In the Network panel, examine how data is loaded, including any API endpoints that may be directly accessed for data retrieval.

Debugging and Overriding: Use the Sources tab to troubleshoot JavaScript bugs and test modifications to the site's codebase.

Using Developer Tools, you may effectively scan web pages, diagnose bugs, and create efficient web scraping programs.

Chapter 9

When should you use APIs vs web scraping?

APIs (Application Programming Interfaces) and web scraping are two popular ways to retrieve data from websites. Each strategy has advantages and disadvantages, and the decision between them is determined by a number of criteria, including data availability, legality, convenience of use, and task-specific needs. Here is a full comparison to help you decide whether to utilize APIs or web scraping.

What are APIs?

APIs are structured interfaces given by websites or services that enable external programs to access certain data or capabilities programmatically. APIs generally output data in formats such as JSON or XML, making it simple to understand and utilize.

Advantages of APIs:

Structured Data: APIs deliver well-organized data.

APIs are less likely to change unexpectedly than HTML structures.

Efficiency: APIs frequently deliver only the data required, minimizing bandwidth and processing time.

Rate restrictions: While restricted, API use restrictions are typically well documented.

Legality: Using an API is typically more legally sound because it is an official method of accessing the service's data.

API disadvantages include the following:

Limited Access: APIs may not provide all of the information accessible on the website.

Rate restrictions: APIs frequently have severe rate restrictions, which limit the quantity of data you may get in a specific time period.

Authorization: Many APIs require API keys or OAuth tokens, which may be obtained by registration and occasionally at a cost.

What is Web Scraping?

Web scraping is the process of programmatically obtaining data from websites by analyzing their HTML content. This may be accomplished with a variety of tools and libraries for navigating and processing web pages.

Advantages of web scraping:

Data Availability: Users may access any data viewable on the webpage, not only what an API exposes.

No Rate Restrictions: APIs are often not constrained by rigid rate restrictions, yet scraping too aggressively may result in being banned.

Flexibility: Can scrape any area of a website, even data that is not available via an API.

The disadvantages of web scraping:

Web scraping programs are fragile and can break if the website's HTML structure changes.

Scraping websites without permission might result in legal troubles since it violates the terms of service.

Bandwidth Intensive: Downloading whole web pages might be more bandwidth intensive than utilizing an API.

Ethical Considerations: Scraping can increase server load, hurting website performance.

When to Use APIs?

When Data is Easily Available: If the data you want is available via an API, it is often preferable to utilize it. APIs are intended to give data in an organized and accessible format.

To ensure stability: APIs are more stable over time than web pages, which can change often.

Legal Compliance: Using an API is typically legally safer because it is the officially sanctioned means of accessing data.

APIs are frequently more efficient for large-scale data collecting since they involve less data transfer and provide more tailored data access.

Rate Limits and Access: If the API's rate limits and data access regulations fit your needs, it makes the procedure easier.

When To Use Web Scraping

Lack of API Access: If no API is accessible or the API does not offer the required data, web scraping may be your only choice.

Data Depth: Scraping can be used to retrieve data that the API does not disclose but is available on the website.

Ad-hoc Data Collection: For one-time or infrequent data collection, using a scraper may be easier than interacting with an API.

Overcoming API Limitations: When API rate limits or data access restrictions are too restrictive, scraping can be used to get around them, but it should be done with caution to prevent being blocked or blacklisted.

Best Practices for both methods.

Regarding APIs:

Read the documentation carefully in order to perform efficient and proper API calls.

Handle Errors Gracefully: Use robust error handling for API rate restrictions and downtime.

Respect Rate restrictions: To prevent being banned, adhere to the rate restrictions and terms of service.

For web scraping:

Respect Robots.txt: Check the website's robots.txt file to see which areas you may scrape.

Throttle Requests: Use rate limitation and random pauses between requests to prevent overloading the server.

Identify Yourself: To identify your bot, use a clear User-Agent string and provide contact information.

manage HTML Changes: Create flexible and resilient parsing code that can manage small changes to the HTML structure.

Keep track of the legal ramifications of scraping, such as copyright laws and terms of service agreements.

Chapter 10

Legal Aspects of Web Scraping

Web scraping, while a great technique for obtaining data from websites, has various legal implications that must be properly negotiated in order to avoid potential problems. The legality of online scraping varies greatly depending on the country, the website's terms of service, and the way the data is utilized.

Here are the main legal factors to consider:

1. Terms of Service (ToS) agreements

Most websites have Terms of Service (ToS) agreements that users must accept. These conditions frequently contain provisions for automated access and data extraction.

Prohibited Actions: Many Terms of Service clearly restrict the use of web scraping or automated bots for data collection.

Binding Agreement: By using the website, users are deemed to have agreed to the TOS. Violating these conditions may result in legal action or a ban from the site.

Example:

If a website's Terms of Service prohibit scraping and you proceed to scrape the site, you may face legal action such as a cease and desist order or a lawsuit for breach of contract.

2. Copyright & Intellectual Property

Copyright and intellectual property regulations frequently protect data and material found on websites.

Content Ownership: A website's content is normally held by the site owner or content author.

Data Use: Unauthorized extraction and use of copyrighted content may constitute copyright infringement.

Example:

Scraping and republishing a whole website's articles without permission is most certainly a blatant infringement of copyright laws.

3. Computer Fraud and Abuse Act (CFAA) - USA

The United States Computer Fraud and Abuse Act (CFAA) is a federal law that forbids unauthorized access to computers and networks:

Unauthorized Access: Under the CFAA, scraping a website in violation of its Terms of Service constitutes unauthorized access.

Legal consequences: Violations of the CFAA can result in civil and criminal sanctions.

Example:

A prominent case concerning the CFAA is LinkedIn v. hiQ Labs, in which LinkedIn claimed that hiQ Labs' scraping of its public profiles violated the CFAA. The case has received various decisions, emphasizing the complexities of interpreting the CFAA in the context of online scraping.

4. General Data Protection Regulation (GDPR) - European Union

The GDPR governs the processing of personal data in the European Union and affects how online scraping can be carried out:

Personal Data: Personal data collected by online scraping must adhere to GDPR criteria such as legitimate basis for processing, data minimization, and transparency.

Individuals have rights to their personal data, including the right to be informed, the right to access, and the right to be erased.

Example:

If you scrape a European website and acquire personal data, you must follow GDPR rules, such as getting consent or demonstrating a legitimate interest in processing the data.

5. Anti-Circumvention laws

Many nations have laws prohibiting the circumvention of technical barriers put in place to protect material.

Circumvention: Using techniques such as CAPTCHA or IP blocking to scrape data may be deemed criminal circumvention.

Penalties: Violating anti-circumvention rules may result in legal action and penalties.

Example:

If a website utilizes CAPTCHA to block automated access and you use a tool to get around it, you may be breaching anti-circumvention laws such as the DMCA (Digital Millennium Copyright Act) in the United States.

6. Case Law and Precedents

Legal precedents and case law significantly influence the legality of web scraping. Courts in numerous countries have made decisions affecting the practice:

Court rulings: Cases such as LinkedIn v. hiQ Labs and eBay v. Bidder's Edge have established key precedents for online scraping.

Jurisdictional Differences: Legal interpretations and results can differ greatly among jurisdictions.

Example:

In the LinkedIn v. hiQ Labs case, the Ninth Circuit Court of Appeals decided in favor of hiQ, holding that scraping public material does not constitute illegal access under the CFAA. However, this judgment is susceptible to change as the legal procedures progress.

Chapter 11

Best Practices to Minimize Legal Risk

To reduce the legal issues related to online scraping, consider the following best practices:

Review ToS Agreements: Always read and follow the website's Terms of Service.

Seek Permission: When feasible, obtain explicit permission from the website owner before scraping.

Avoid Sensitive Data: Do not scrape personal or other data that is protected by privacy regulations.

Respect robots.txt: Follow the directions in the website's robots.txt file, which specifies which portions of the site may be viewed by web crawlers.

Implement Ethical Scraping: Use rate restriction and avoid overloading the website's server to reduce disturbance.

Legal Consultation: Speak with a legal professional to better understand the legal ramifications and ensure compliance with applicable laws and regulations.

Respecting the Website Terms of Service

Respecting a website's Terms of Service (ToS) is an important part of web scraping for legal compliance and ethical behavior. The Terms of Service explain the rules and instructions for accessing the website, and they frequently contain terms governing automated access and data extraction. Here's how to properly respect and comply with a website's Terms of Service when scraping data:

Understanding the Terms of Service

Terms of Service (ToS), often known as Terms of Use or User Agreement, are legally binding agreements between the website operator and the user. They specify the allowed uses of the website and its content. Violating the Terms of Service might result in legal repercussions and access limitations.

Key Features to Look For

When examining a website's Terms of Service, pay attention to the following crucial provisions:

Automated Access Restrictions: Many websites expressly ban the use of bots, spiders, or other automated means to access or extract data.

Data Usage and Redistribution: Some Terms of Service stipulate how data from the website may be used or redistributed. This may include prohibitions on commercial usage or sharing of scraped data.

Rate Limiting and Access Frequency: Guidelines for how frequently requests can be sent to the website to avoid server overload.

material Ownership and Copyright: Clauses governing the ownership of the website's material, as well as limits on copying and reusing it.

Privacy and Personal Data: Provisions governing the acquisition, use, and protection of personal data, which are particularly critical for ensuring compliance with data protection legislation such as GDPR.

Steps to Respect the Terms of Service

Before beginning any web scraping project, read and understand the Terms of Service. Look for parts that discuss automated access, scraping, data usage, and legal limits.

Seek Permission: If the Terms of Service are confusing or forbid scraping, contact the website's owner to request permission. A formal request detailing the aim of the data extraction and how you intend to utilize the data may result in access being granted.

Check the website's robots.txt file, which specifies which portions of the site may be viewed by web crawlers. While not legally required, following robots.txt is considered good practice and indicates respect for the website's preferences.

Chapter 12

Implement ethical scraping practices:

Rate limitation: Use rate limitation to avoid overloading the server with too many requests in a short time.

Politeness: Create unpredictable pauses between queries to simulate human browsing behavior.

User-Agent Identification: Use a distinct and easily recognizable User-Agent string, and avoid mimicking other browsers or users.

Respectful Data Extraction: Only extract the data you need, without scraping unnecessary or excessive data.

Compliance with Legal Regulations: Ensure that your scraping operations adhere to applicable legal rules, such as copyright and data protection laws (e.g., GDPR).

Monitor for Changes: Keep an eye out for changes to the website's Terms of Service. Websites have the ability to amend their Terms of Service, and being up to current on the newest terms is critical for compliance.

Example ToS Clauses

Here are some examples of popular Terms of Service terms for web scraping:

Prohibition of Automated Access

"You agree not to use any robot, spider, scraper, or other automated means to access the Website for any purpose without our express written permission."

Restrictions on data use:

"You may not copy, modify, distribute, or sell any content from the Website without our prior written consent."

Rate Limiting:

"You agree not to make more than X requests to the Website within any 24-hour period."

Content Ownership:

"All content on the Website is owned by [Website Owner] and is protected by copyright and other intellectual property laws."

Personal Data Protection:

"You agree not to collect or store personal data about other users of the Website."

Consequences of Violating Terms of Service

Violating a website's Terms of Service can have various consequences:

Account Suspension or Ban: If the website needs user registration, your account may be suspended or blocked.

Legal Action: The website owner may file a lawsuit against you for breach of contract, copyright infringement, or illegal access under laws such as the CFAA in the United States.

Cease and desist orders: You may receive a cease and desist order requiring you to stop scraping the website and destroy all data acquired.

IP Blocking: The website may block your IP address, limiting future access to the site.

When performing online scraping, it is critical to adhere to the Terms of Service of the website. You may guarantee that your online scraping operations are legally compliant and respectful of the website owner's standards by carefully examining the Terms of Service, obtaining permission where necessary, following robots.txt guidelines, and using ethical scraping techniques. This strategy not only helps to avoid legal concerns but also develops strong relationships with website owners, which may lead to more chances for data access in the future.

Chapter 13

Best practices for ethical scraping

Ethical online scraping entails following legal and ethical principles to minimize the harmful effects on websites and their owners when gathering data. Here are the recommended methods for doing your web scraping activity properly and ethically:

1. Follow the Terms of Service (ToS).

Read and Understand the Terms of Service: Always review the website's Terms of Service to see if there are any limits on automatic data extraction.

Seek Permission: If scraping is forbidden, consider contacting the website owner and requesting express permission.

2. Follow the robots.txt directives.

Check robots.txt: Examine the website's robots.txt file to see whether portions of the site are accessible to web spiders.

Follow the Guidelines: To prevent visiting forbidden locations, follow the guidelines in the robots.txt file.

3. Implement Rate Limiting and Throttling.

Limit Request Frequency: To avoid overwhelming the server, try not to make too many requests in a short period of time.

Randomize Delays: Use unpredictable delays between requests to mimic human browsing activity and lessen the probability of being banned.

4. Identify yourself. Clearly

Use a Clear User-Agent: Make sure your requests contain a clear and recognizable User-Agent string. Do not use misleading or generic User-Agent strings.

Contact Information: Optionally, put contact information in the User-Agent string or headers so that website owners can contact you if there are any problems.

5. Concentrate on the data you need.

Targeted Scraping: Extract just the data required for your project. Avoid collecting excessive or useless data.

Minimize Load: Limit the quantity of data you download to reduce the effect on the site's bandwidth and resources.

6. Handle errors. Gracefully

Implement Error Handling: Make sure your scraping script can handle HTTP failures, network problems, and server outages gracefully.

Respect rate limits. If the website has rate constraints, make your scraper comply with them.

7. Respect privacy and data protection.

Avoid Personal Data: Scrape personal data only when absolutely required, and follow privacy requirements such as GDPR.

Data Anonymization: If personal information must be obtained, anonymize it to safeguard people's privacy.

8. Legal Compliance.

If you're unclear about the legality of your scrapping project, get legal counsel to guarantee compliance with relevant laws and regulations.

9. Track Website Changes

Adapt to Changes: Websites' structures and terms of service may change over time. Monitor and update your scraper on a regular basis to keep up with the latest updates.

Error Detection: Set up systems to identify changes in the website structure that may influence your scraping operation.

10. Be transparent and accountable.

Disclose Scraping Activities: If possible, notify the website owner of your scraping operations and the objective of data capture.

Transparency With Users: If you're gathering data for public or third-party use, be open about the sources and verify accuracy and dependability.

11. Utilize ethical scraping tools and libraries.

Select Reputable Tools: Use well-known and reliable web scraping tools and libraries that are intended to have little impact on websites.

Contribute back: If you can, help the community by sharing best practices, reporting issues, and developing scraping tools.

12. Respect Intellectual Property Attribute Content: When using scraped content publicly, credit the original source whenever applicable.

Avoid Copyright Infringement: Do not scrape or reuse copyrighted information in a manner that breaches copyright laws.

13. Data Use and Ethics.

Use Data properly: Scraped data should be handled properly and ethically, with no malevolent intent.

Avoid exploitation. Ensure that the data is not utilized to exploit or damage persons or organizations.

Example scenario: Ethical Scraping in Practice

Assume you wish to scrape product reviews from an e-commerce website to examine customer sentiment. Here's how you can implement ethical scraping practices:

Review the website's Terms of Service to confirm that scraping reviews is authorized. If not clearly authorized, request permission from the website's owner.

Check Robots.txt: Make sure the robots.txt file allows you to access the reviews area.

Rate Limiting and Throttling: Set your scraper to send no more than one request per few seconds. Use random delays to simulate human browsing.

Identify yourself: Use a clear User-Agent string, such as MyScraperBot/1.0 (+contact@example.com).

Targeted Data Extraction: Only extract the review text, rating, and date, omitting irrelevant data such as photographs or user profiles.

Error Handling: Use error handling to address possible problems like as 404 errors and server unavailability.

Privacy Compliance: Unless absolutely essential and legally required, do not gather personal information from reviews, such as usernames or profile images.

lawful Compliance: Consult a lawyer to confirm that your scraping actions are lawful.

**Monitor

Website Changes: Check the website on a regular basis for changes to the structure or terms of service, and update your scraper accordingly.

Transparency and accountability: When publishing your study, identify the data source and method of gathering. Ensure that your results are accurate and provide proper credit to the data source.

Use Ethical Tools: Use respected scraping libraries such as BeautifulSoup or Scrapy, and consider providing enhancements to the community.

Respect Intellectual Property: If you include reviews in your analysis, make sure to attribute them to the original source and follow any usage limitations.

Responsible Data Usage: Use the information gathered from the evaluations in a responsible manner, providing constructive comments or improving services rather than harming rivals or manipulating public opinion.

Ethical online scraping requires a delicate combination of technological expertise, legal understanding, and respect for the website and its owners. By adhering to these best practices, you may guarantee that your online scraping operations are responsible, legally compliant, and respectful of data integrity and website resources. This strategy not only helps to avoid legal and ethical issues but also promotes strong connections with website owners and the larger community.

Chapter 14

Installation and Configuration for Web Scraping

Getting started with web scraping entails creating your development environment, installing the essential tools and libraries, and ensuring that your machine is properly equipped for scraping tasks. Here's a step-by-step tutorial to take you through the installation and configuration procedure.

1. Setting up your development environment.

1.1. Select a programming language.

Python is the most often used language for online scraping due to its simplicity and the availability of sophisticated tools such as BeautifulSoup, Scrapy, and Selenium.

1.2. Install Python.

Windows:

Get the Python installation from the official Python website.

Run the installation, and make sure to tick the option to add Python to your PATH.

To verify the installation, open a command line and type python --version.

MacOS:

Open the terminal.

If you haven't previously, install Homebrew with: /bin/bash   -c   "$(curl   -fsSL https://raw.githubusercontent.com/Homebrew/install/HEAD/install.sh)".

Install Python with Homebrew: brew install python.

Run the python3 --version to verify the installation.

Linux:

Open the terminal.

Use the package manager of your distribution (e.g., apt for Ubuntu): sudo apt update and sudo apt install python3.

To verify the installation, execute python3 --version. 1.3. Create a Virtual Environment

Using a virtual environment allows you to manage dependencies and separate your projects.

Install virtualenv: pip install virtualenv.

Create a virtual environment (virtualenv myenv).

To activate the virtual environment on Windows, navigate to myenv\Scripts\activate. For MacOS/Linux, use the source command. myenv/bin/activate

2. Installing Web Scraping Libraries.

2.1. Install BeautifulSoup.

BeautifulSoup is a package that parses HTML and XML documents.

Install beautifulsoup4 and lxml using pip. Then, install Requests (2.2).

Request is a library for creating HTTP requests.

Pip install requests 2.3. Install Scrapy

Scrapy is an open-source platform for performing large-scale web scraping.

Install Scrappy using pip. Then, install Selenium version 2.4.

Selenium automates web browsers, making it helpful for harvesting dynamic material.

To install Selenium, use pip and WebDriver.

For Chrome, download ChromeDriver and save it in a location on your system's PATH.

To move ChromeDriver on MacOS/Linux: sudo mv chrome driver/usr/local/bin/ 2.5. Install additional libraries.

Install other useful libraries as required, such as Pandas for data manipulation.

pip install pandas

3. Creating Your First Scraping Script 3.1. Implementing BeautifulSoup and Requests

Create the script scrape.py:

Python: import requests from bs4 import BeautifulSoup

Scrape URL: 'http://example.com'

Send a GET request. Response = requests.get(url) response.raise_for_status() # Check for request errors.

Parse HTML content soup = BeautifulSoup(response.content, 'lxml').

Extract data (e.g. all paragraph texts)

Paragraphs are the same as soup. To detect all occurrences of 'p' within paragraphs, use the following code:

```
print(p.get_text())
```

3.2. Using Scraps

Create a scrappy project:

Scrapy Start Project My Project

Navigate to the project directory and create a spider.

cd my-project scrappy genspider.example.com

Edit the produced spider in myproject/spiders/example.py.

Python: import scrappy.

Class ExampleSpider (scrappy. Spider):

Name: 'example' Start URLs: ['http://example.com']

define parse(self, response): for p in response.CSS('p'): return {'text': p.get()}

Run the spider. Run the following command in the terminal: # Scrapy crawl example.

4. Testing & Debugging

4.1. Use the Browser Developer Tools.

Inspect components and network activity with tools such as Chrome Developer Tools to better understand the structure of the webpage and the requests being sent.

4.2. Use logging.

Add logging to your scripts to help you diagnose problems and keep track of scraping activity.

Python imports logging.

logging.basicConfig(level=logging.INFO)

logger = logging.getLogger(__name__).

Example usage: logger.info('Starting scraping...')

5. Staying Up to Date

5.1. Regularly update libraries.

Keep your libraries and tools up to current so you can take advantage of the most recent features and security upgrades.

pip install --upgrade. Beautifulsoup4 Requests Scrapy Selenium 5.2. Follow Community Guidelines.

Stay up to date on best practices and legal issues by engaging with the web scraping community via forums, blogs, and official documentation.

Following these steps will provide a good basis for web scraping with popular technologies such as

BeautifulSoup, Scrapy, and Selenium. Ensuring correct installation and setup is critical for efficient and successful web scraping, allowing you to concentrate on obtaining and analyzing the data you want.

Chapter 15

Navigating HTML Documents

Navigating HTML web pages is a necessary skill in web scraping since it entails obtaining particular data from online sites. This approach usually entails studying the structure of HTML and utilizing tools like BeautifulSoup to find and extract the needed information.

1. Understanding HTML structure.

HTML is the standard language for building web pages. It organizes material via tags, attributes, and hierarchical components. Here are the basic components.

Tags define elements in HTML documents (e.g., <div>, <p>, <a>).

Attributes: Provide more information about items (such as class, ID, and link).

Nested Elements: Elements can be nested inside other elements to form a hierarchical structure.

Example HTML structure:

html

Copy the code: <!DOCTYPE html> <html> <head> <title>Example Page</title> </head> <body> <h1>Heading:</h1> <p class="intro">This is an opening paragraph.</p> <div id="content"> <p class="text">This is a paragraph within a division.</p> <a href="http://example.com" class="link">.Example link: <a> </div> </body> </html>

2. Using BeautifulSoup to Parse HTML

BeautifulSoup is a robust Python package for parsing HTML and XML documents. It offers techniques for traversing and searching the parse tree.

Installation:

To create a BeautifulSoup object, follow these steps: - Copy the code - Install beautifulsoup4 lxml - Create the object

python

Copy the code from bs4 and import BeautifulSoup.

HTML_content = """ <!DOCTYPE html> <html> <head> <title>Example Page</title> </head> <body> <h1>Heading:</h1> <p class="intro">This is an opening paragraph.</p> <div id="content"> <p class="text">This is a paragraph within a division.</p> <a href="http://example.com" class="link">.Example link: <a> </div> </body> </html>soup= BeautifulSoup(html_content, 'lxml').

3. Parse Tree Navigation: Accessing Elements by Tag.

Python

Find the first `<h1>`. `h1_tag = soup.find('h1')print(h1_tag.get_text())`

Find All Elements by Tag:

python

To discover all `<p>` tags, use `p_tags = soup.find_all('p')`. Then, for each p in `p_tags:print(p.get_text())`

Using Attributes to Find Elements:

Python

Find the first `<p>`. Tag with class "intro":`intro_p=soup.find('p',class_='intro').print(intro_p.get_text())`

Locate the `<div>` tag with the id "content".

The content_div is `soup.Find('div', id='content')`

`print(content_div.get_text())` CSS selector:

Use CSS selectors to find elements: `intro_p = soup.select_one('p.intro')`.

```python
print(intro_p.get_text())
```

Links equal soup. Select 'a.link' and look for the link under links.

```python
Print(link.get_text(), link['href'])
```

4. Using the HTML Tree: Parent and Sibling Navigation.

Python

Navigate to Parent.Parent_div = intro_p.find_parent('div').print(parent_div)

Navigate to the next sibling: next_sibling = intro_p.find_next_sibling('p').

```python
print(next_sibling.get_text())
```

Children and descendants:

python

Copy code: #. To obtain the children of a tag, use the following code: content_children =

content_div.findChildren() for child in content_children: print(child. name, child.get_text()).

To retrieve the descendants of a tag, use the following code: content_descendants = content_div.find_all() for descendant in content_descendants: print(descendant.name, descendant.get_text()).

5. Extracting Data from Attributes.

Getting Attribute Values:

Python

Copy code: #. Extract the href property from the <a> tag: link = soup.find('a', class = 'link')

print(link['href'])

Handling Missing attributes:

To prevent a KeyError if an attribute is missing, use the get method with link_href set to link.GET('href', 'No href attribute')

print(link_href)

Example: Scraping a real webpage

Here's an example of scraping a real web page with BeautifulSoup and Requests:

Import requests From bs4 import BeautifulSoup

Web page URL to scrape: url = 'http://example.com'.

Make an HTTP GET request to the URL. response = requests.get(url) response.raise_for_status() # Make sure the request was successful.

Parse the page's HTML content using BeautifulSoup(response.content, 'lxml').

Extract the page title page_title = soup.title.string print('Page Title:', page_title)

Extract all the paragraph texts.

Paragraphs are the same as soup. To detect all occurrences of 'p' within paragraphs, use the following code: print(p.get_text())

To extract all links containing URLs, use the following code: links = soup.find_all('a', href=True) For each link in links: Print(link.get_text(), link['href'])

Successful web scraping requires the ability to successfully navigate HTML content. Understanding HTML structure, as well as employing tools like BeautifulSoup, helps you to easily discover and extract data. By learning these approaches, you may create powerful scrapers that extract important information from websites.

Chapter 16

Extracting Data with BeautifulSoup

BeautifulSoup is a sophisticated Python package that helps you extract data from HTML and XML texts. Here's a full guide on extracting data with BeautifulSoup:

1. Setup BeautifulSoup Installation:

To create a BeautifulSoup object, follow these steps: - Copy the code - Install beautifulsoup4 lxml - Create the object

from bs4 and import BeautifulSoup.

HTML_content = """ <!DOCTYPE html> <html> <head> <title>Example Page</title> </head> <body> <h1>Heading:</h1> <p class="intro">This is an opening paragraph.</p> <div id="content"> <p class="text">This is a paragraph within a division.</p> <a href="http://example.com"

class="link">.Example link: <a> </div> </body> </html>soup = BeautifulSoup(html_content, 'lxml').

2. Basic Extraction Techniques

Find Elements by Tag Name:

python

Find the first <h1>. h1_tag = soup.find('h1')

print(h1_tag.get_text())

Find All Elements by Tag Name:

To discover all <p> tags, use p_tags = soup.find_all('p'). Then, for each p in p_tags:print(p.get_text())

Finding Elements by Attribute:

Find the first <p>. Tag with class "intro": intro_p = soup.find('p', class_='intro').

print(intro_p.get_text())

Locate the <div> tag with the id "content"
content_div = soup.Find('div', id='content')

print(content_div.get_text())

3. Applying CSS Selectors

CSS selectors offer a strong method for locating elements:

Use CSS selectors to find elements: intro_p = soup.select_one('p.intro').

print(intro_p.get_text())

Links equal soup.Select 'a.link' and look for the link under links.

Print(link.get_text(), link['href'])

4. Using the HTML Tree: Parent and Sibling Navigation.

Navigate to Parent.

Parent_div = intro_p.find_parent('div').

```python
print(parent_div)
```

Navigate to the next sibling: next_sibling = intro_p.find_next_sibling('p').

```python
print(next_sibling.get_text())
```

Children and descendants:

To obtain the children of a tag, use the following code: content_children = content_div.findChildren() for child in content_children: print(child. name, child.get_text()).

To retrieve the descendants of a tag, use the following code: content_descendants = content_div.find_all() for descendant in content_descendants: print(descendant. name, descendant.get_text()).

5. Extracting Data from Attributes.

Getting Attribute Values:

Extract the href property from the <a> tag: link = soup.find('a', class = 'link')

print(link['href'])

Handling Missing attributes:

To prevent a KeyError if an attribute is missing, use the get method with link_href set to link.GET('href', 'No href attribute')

print(link_href)

6. Example: Scraping a real web page.

Here's an example of scraping a real web page with BeautifulSoup and Requests:

Import requests From bs4 import BeautifulSoup

Web page URL to scrape: url = 'http://example.com'.

Make an HTTP GET request to the URL. response = requests.get(url) response.raise_for_status() # Make sure the request was successful.

Parse the page's HTML content using BeautifulSoup(response.content, 'lxml').

Extract the page title page_title = soup.title.string print('Page Title:', page_title)

Extract all the paragraph texts.

Paragraphs are the same as soup. To detect all occurrences of 'p' within paragraphs, use the following code:print(p.get_text())

To extract all links containing URLs, use the following code: links = soup.find_all('a', href=True) For each link in links:

Print(link.get_text(),link['href'])

7. Advanced Techniques for Extracting Tables:

Python Copy code html_table = "" "<table> <tr> <th>Name</th>   <th>Age</th>   </tr>   <tr>

```
<td>Alice</td>     <td>30</td>     </tr>     <tr>
<td>Bob</td> <td>25</td> </tr> </table>soup =
BeautifulSoup(html_table, 'lxml').
```

```
# Extract table headers: headers =
[header.get_text() for header in
soup.find_all('th')].
```

```
print(headers)
```

```
# Extract table rows.
```

```
Rows = [] for each row in the soup.find_all('tr')[1:]:
Columns = row.find_all('td')
Rows.append([column.get_text() for column in
columns].
```

```
print(rows)
```

Handling JavaScript-Rendered Content

For JavaScript-rendered content, use Selenium to
control a browser and extract the HTML.

from Selenium and import it into WebDriver.

```
# Configure Selenium WebDriver driver =
webdriver.Chrome()

# Access the web page:
driver.get('http://example.com')

# Extract the page content.

html_content = driver.page_source; soup =
BeautifulSoup(html_content, 'lxml').

# Close the browser driver.quit()

# Now you may continue using BeautifulSoup as
normal.
```

BeautifulSoup is a flexible tool for extracting information from HTML files. By knowing its different capabilities and strategies, you will be able to easily explore and scrape data from websites. Whether you're working with simple static material or more complicated dynamic sites, BeautifulSoup, when paired with additional tools like Requests and Selenium, provides a powerful solution for online scraping.

Chapter 17

Handling JavaScript-generated Content

Many current websites use JavaScript to dynamically load information, making it difficult to scrape data with old approaches. To handle JavaScript-rendered content, technologies such as Selenium or Pyppeteer may be used to interact with web pages in the same way a browser would. Here's how you can utilize these tools to scrape such material.

1. Using Selenium

Selenium is an extremely effective technology for automating web browsers. It can interface with websites, run JavaScript, and extract dynamically loaded material.

pip install selenium

Setup WebDriver:

Download the WebDriver for your browser (such as ChromeDriver for Chrome).

Ensure that the WebDriver executable is in your system's PATH.

Example Script:

from Selenium import web driver.

From selenium.webdriver.common.by import By.

From selenium.webdriver.chrome.service import Service.

From selenium.webdriver.chrome.options import Options.

From webdriver_manager.chrome, import ChromeDriverManager.

From bs4 import BeautifulSoup.

Import Time

Set up Chrome preferences.

Chrome_options = Options().

```
chrome_options.add_argument("--headless")     #
Use headless mode.

# Setup Chrome WebDriver

Service                                       =
Service(ChromeDriverManager().install())

Driver:        webdriver.Chrome(service=service,
options=chrome_options)

# URL of the webpage to scrape.

url: 'http://example.com'

# Open the webpage.

driver.get(URL)

# Wait for the webpage to load.

time. sleep(5)

# Adjust this according to the page loading time

# Extract the page source.

HTML_content equals driver.page_source.

# Close your browser.

driver.quit()
```

```
# Parse the HTML content using BeautifulSoup.

soup = BeautifulSoup(html_content, 'lxml').

# Extract the desired data.

page_title equals soup. title.string

Print('Page Title:', page_title)

Paragraphs = soup.find_all('p').

For p in paragraphs:

print(p.get_text())
```

2. Using Puppeteer.

Puppeteer is a Python port of Puppeteer that runs a headless version of Chrome or Chromium.

Installation:

pip install pyppeteer.

Example Script:

```
import asyncio.

from Python, import launch

From bs4 import BeautifulSoup.


asynchronous def main():

# Launch a headless browser.

Browser = await launch (headless=True)

page = await browser.newPage().


# URL of the webpage to scrape.

url: 'http://example.com'


# Open the webpage.

await page.goto(url).


# Wait for the material to load.
```

```
await page.waitForSelector('p')  # Change this
depending on the content you're waiting for.

# Extract page content.

html_content = await page.content().

# Close your browser.

await browser.close().

# Parse the HTML content using BeautifulSoup.

soup = BeautifulSoup(html_content, 'lxml').

# Extract the desired data.

page_title equals soup.title.string

Print('Page Title:', page_title)

Paragraphs = soup.find_all('p').

For p in paragraphs:

print(p.get_text())

# Run the script.

asyncio.get_event_loop().run_until_complete(main())
```

3. Tips for Effectively Scraping JavaScript-rendered Content

Waiting for content to load.

To suspend execution for a specific amount of time, call time.sleep().

Use Selenium's WebDriverWait method to wait for certain components to load.

From selenium.webdriver.common.by import By.

Selenium.webdriver.support.ui import WebDriverWait

From selenium.webdriver.support import expected_conditions as EC.

Example of waiting for an element to appear

element = WebDriverWait(driver, 10).until()

EC.presence_of_element_located(By.ID, 'element_id'))

Handling infinite scrolling:

To simulate scrolling, send JavaScript commands to the browser.

Scroll to the bottom of the page.

Driver.execute_script("window.scrollTo(0, document.body.scrollHeight);"

time.sleep(5) # Wait for fresh content to load.

Dealing with pop-ups and modals:

Close pop-ups and modals by clicking their close buttons.

Close the modal or pop-up

Close_button = driver.find_element(By.CLASS_NAME, 'close-button-class').

close_button.click()

Selenium and Pyppeteer are powerful tools that allow you to scrape data from modern web applications that use JavaScript to load content. These tools are capable of executing JavaScript and interacting with dynamic web pages.

Chapter 18

Advanced Methods for Dynamic Content Extraction

When working with complicated websites that mainly rely on JavaScript to load material dynamically, more advanced strategies are required. Here are some advanced techniques for extracting dynamic content using Selenium and other tools.

1. Handle JavaScript Execution

Waiting for Javascript to execute:

You can use JavaScript itself or wait for particular circumstances to confirm that JavaScript has finished executing and that the material has fully loaded.

Example:

From selenium.webdriver.common.by import By.

Selenium.webdriver.support.ui import WebDriverWait

From selenium.webdriver.support import expected_conditions as EC.

Wait till the element is present.

element = WebDriverWait(driver, 10).until()

EC.presence_of_element_located((By.ID, 'dynamic_element_id').)

Custom Javascript Execution:

Run custom JavaScript to guarantee that all data is loaded.

driver.execute_script(Returndocument.readyState 'complete'.)

2. Interact with Elements

Filling up and submitting forms:

To scrape data that needs a form submit.

Example:

Find the form components and submit.

```
Search box = driver.find_element(By.NAME, 'q')

search_box.send_keys("example query")

search_box.submit()
```

Handling dropdowns and checkboxes:

```
from selenium.webdriver.support.UI import
```

Choose an option from the dropdown

```
dropdown = Select(driver.find_element(By.ID, 'dropdown_id').

dropdown.select_by_visible_text("Option Text").
```

Click a checkbox.

```
Checkbox = driver.find_element(By.ID, 'checkbox_id')

checkbox.click()
```

3. Managing pop-ups, alerts, and frames.

Closing Pop-ups:

Switch to the alert and accept it.

Alert = driver.switch_to.alert.

alert.accept()

Handling Frames:

To interact with components within frames.

Example:

Navigate to a frame by name or ID

driver.switch_to.frame('frame_name_or_id')

Go back to the default content

driver.switch_to.default_content()

4. Taking screenshots

Taking screenshots can be beneficial for troubleshooting and data collection.

Example:

Save a screenshot of the current page.

driver.save_screenshot('screenshot.png')

5. Scraping infinite scrolling pages.

Infinite scrolling sites load more material as you scroll down. Here's a reliable method:

Example:

Last_height = driver.execute_script("return document.body.scrollHeight").

While True:

Scroll to the bottom.

Driver.execute_script("window.scrollTo(0, document.body.scrollHeight);"

time.sleep(5) # Wait for fresh content to load.

Calculate the new scroll height and compare it to the previous height.

new_height = driver.execute_script("Return document.body.scrollHeight").

If new_height equals last_height:

break

Last_height equals new_height

6. Extracting data from single-page applications.

SPAs dynamically refresh the page's content without requiring a full reload; use Selenium to interact with these pages in the same way a user would.

Example:

Click a button to load further material.

load_more_button = driver.find_element(By.ID,'load_more_button').

load_more_button.click()time.sleep (5) Wait for the content to load.

7. Using Headless Browsers.

Running browsers in headless mode (without a GUI) can help speed up the scraping process.

Headless mode in Chrome:

From selenium.webdriver.chrome.options import Options.

Options = Options().

options.add_argument("--headless")

Driver: webdriver.Chrome(options=options)

8. Using Proxies and User Agents.

To evade detection and blockage by websites, utilize proxies and change your user agent.

Setting   Proxies:from selenium.webdriver.common.proxy import Proxy, ProxyType.proxy=Proxy();proxy.proxy_type   is ProxyType.MANUAL.proxy.http_proxy: 'http://your_proxy:port'Proxy.ssl_proxy   = 'http://your_proxy:port'

capabilities: webdriver.Desired capabilities.CHROME

proxy.add_to_capabilities(capabilities)

Driver = webdriver.Chrome(desired_capabilities=capabilities).

Modifying user agents:Options = Options().options.add_argument("user-agent=Mozilla/5.0 (Windows NT 10.0; Win64; x64) AppleWebKit/537.36 (KHTML, like Gecko) Chrome/91.0.4472.124 Safari/537.36")

Driver: webdriver.Chrome(options=options)

9. Capturing Network Traffic

To collect network data and analyze API calls, use browser developer tools such as Selenium Wire.

Selenium Wire:

from SeleniumWire import webdriver

Driver = webdriver.Chrome().

```
# Access requests via the driver.requests property.

driver.get('http://example.com')

for request in driver.requests.

If request.response:

print(request.url, response.status_code, headers)
```

10. Scraping data with Pyppeteer

Pyppeteer provides greater control over headless browsers.

Example:

```
import asyncio.

from Python, import launch

asynchronous def main():

Browser = await launch (headless=True)

page = await browser.newPage().

await page.goto('http://example.com').
```

```
await
page.waitForSelector('#dynamic_element_id').

content = await page.content().

await browser.close().

print(content)

asyncio.get_event_loop().run_until_complete(mai
n())
```

Advanced dynamic content extraction necessitates handling JavaScript execution, user interactions, infinite scrolling, and more. You can effectively scrape data from complex, modern web applications by using Selenium, Pyppeteer, and other techniques such as modifying user agents and capturing network traffic.

Chapter 19

Parsing the extracted data

After you've extracted HTML content with tools like Selenium or Pyppeteer, you'll need to parse it to get the information you need. Common methods for parsing HTML content include BeautifulSoup, lxml, and regular expressions (regex). Here's a step-by-step guide to effectively parsing extracted data.

1. Using BeautifulSoup.

Installation:

pip install beautifulsoup4 lxml.

Create a BeautifulSoup Object:

From bs4 import BeautifulSoup.HTML_content =<!DOCTYPE HTML><html><head>Title: Example Page</head><body><h1>Heading</h1>

This is an opening paragraph.

```
<div id="content">.<p class="text">A paragraph within a div.</p><a href="http://example.com"class="link">Anexampl elink</a>.</div></body></html>
```

soup = BeautifulSoup(html_content, 'lxml').

2. Finding the Elements

Find Elements by Tag Name:

```
h1_tag = soup.find("h1").
print(h1_tag.get_text())
```

Find All Elements by Tag Name:

```
p_tags = soup.find_all("p").
For p in p_tags:
print(p.get_text())
```

Finding Elements by Attribute:

```
intro_p = soup.find('p', class = 'intro')

print(intro_p.get_text())

Content_Div = soup.find('div', id='content')

print(content_div.get_text())
```

3. Applying CSS Selectors

CSS selectors are an effective approach to locating components in HTML.

Example:

```
Intro_p = soup.select_one('p.intro')

print(intro_p.get_text())

Links = soup.select('a.link')

For the link in links:

Print(link.get_text(), link['href'])
```

4. Navigating the HTML Tree

Parental and Sibling Navigation:

Parent_div = intro_p.find_parent('div').

print(parent_div)

Next_sibling = intro_p.find_next_sibling('p').

print(next_sibling.get_text())

Children and descendants:

Content_children = content_div.findChildren().

For the kid in content_children:

Print (child.name, child.get_text())

Content_descendants = content_div.find_all()

For descendant in content_descendants:

Print (descendant.name, descendant.get_text())

5. Extracting Data from Attributes.

Getting Attribute Values:

Link = soup.find('a', class_='link')print(link['href'])

Handling Missing Attributes:

link_href = link.get('href', 'No href attribute').

print(link_href)

6. Parsing Tables.

Example:

HTML_Table
"""<table><tr><th>Name</th><th>Age</th></tr>
<tr><td>Alice</td><td>30</td></tr><tr><td>Bob</td><td>25</td></tr></table>soup=BeautifulSoup(
html_table, 'lxml').# Extract table headers.

Headers = [header.get_text() for header in
soup.find_all('th')].

print(headers)

Extract table rows.

rows = []

For each row in soup.find_all('tr')[1:]:

Columns = row.find_all('td').

rows.append([column.get_text() for column in columns].

print(rows)

7. Using LXML.

Installation:

pip install lxml.

Parsing with LXML:

From lxml import html.

HTML_content =<!DOCTYPE HTML><html><head>

Title: Example Page

</head><body><h1>Heading</h1>

This is an opening paragraph.

```
<div id="content">.<p class="text">A paragraph within a div.</p>

<a href="http://example.com" class="link">An example link</a>.</div></body>

</html>


Tree = HTML.fromstring(html_content)

# Extracting elements.

h1_text = tree.xpath('//h1/text()', [0]

print(h1_text)

p_texts = tree.xpath('//p/text()').

For text in p_texts:

print(text)


# Extracting characteristics.

Links = tree.xpath('//a/@href').

For the link in links:

print(link)
```

8. Using Regular Expressions.

Regex may be used to extract certain patterns of data from HTML text.

Example:

Import re

HTML_content = """<html><body>

This is an opening paragraph.

<p class="text">A paragraph within a div.</p></body></html>"""

Find all paragraph texts.

Paragraphs = re.findall(r'<p class=".*?"">(.*?)</p>" (html_content)

For p in paragraphs:

print(p)

Using tools like BeautifulSoup, lxml, and regular expressions, you can effectively navigate and extract the information you need from HTML content. Each tool has its own strengths, and selecting the right one depends on the complexity of the task and your specific needs. With these techniques, you can efficiently process and analyze data from multiple web sources.

Chapter 20

Handling JavaScript-generated Content

Many current websites use JavaScript to dynamically load information, making it difficult to scrape data with old approaches. To handle JavaScript-rendered content, technologies such as Selenium or Pyppeteer may be used to interact with web pages in the same way a browser would. Here's how you can utilize these tools to scrape such material.

1. Using Selenium

Selenium is an extremely effective technology for automating web browsers. It can interface with websites, run JavaScript, and extract dynamically loaded material.

Installation:

pip install selenium

Setup WebDriver:

Download the WebDriver for your browser (such as ChromeDriver for Chrome).

Ensure that the WebDriver executable is in your system's PATH.

Example Script:

```
from Selenium import webdriver.

From selenium.webdriver.common.by import By.

From selenium.webdriver.chrome.service import Service.

From selenium.webdriver.chrome.options import Options.

From webdriver_manager.chrome, import ChromeDriverManager.

From bs4 import BeautifulSoup.
```

Import Time

Set up Chrome preferences.

```
Chrome_options = Options().

chrome_options.add_argument("--headless")    #
Use headless mode.

# Setup Chrome WebDriver

Service                                      =
Service(ChromeDriverManager().install())

Driver:        webdriver.Chrome(service=service,
options=chrome_options)

# URL of the webpage to scrape.

url: 'http://example.com'

# Open the webpage.

driver.get(URL)

# Wait for the webpage to load.

time.sleep(5) # Adjust this according to the page
loading time

# Extract the page source.

HTML_content equals driver.page_source.

# Close your browser.
```

```
driver.quit()

# Parse the HTML content using BeautifulSoup.

soup = BeautifulSoup(html_content, 'lxml').

# Extract the desired data.

page_title equals soup.title.string

Print('Page Title:', page_title)


Paragraphs = soup.find_all('p').

For p in paragraphs:

print(p.get_text())
```

2. Using Pyppeteer.

Pyppeteer is a Python port of Puppeteer that runs a headless version of Chrome or Chromium.

Installation:

pip install pyppeteer.

Example Script:

```
import asyncio.

from Python, import launch

From bs4 import BeautifulSoup.

asynchronous def main():

# Launch a headless browser.

Browser = await launch (headless=True)

page = await browser.newPage().

# URL of the webpage to scrape.

url: 'http://example.com'

# Open the webpage.

await page.goto(url).

# Wait for the material to load.

await page.waitForSelector('p')  # Change this
depending on the content you're waiting for.

# Extract page content.

html_content = await page.content().
```

```python
# Close your browser.

await browser.close().

# Parse the HTML content using BeautifulSoup.

soup = BeautifulSoup(html_content, 'lxml').

# Extract the desired data.

page_title equals soup.title.string

Print('Page Title:', page_title)

Paragraphs = soup.find_all('p').

For p in paragraphs:

print(p.get_text())


# Run the script.

asyncio.get_event_loop().run_until_complete(main())
```

3. Tips for Effectively Scraping JavaScript-rendered Content

Waiting for content to load.

To suspend execution for a specific amount of time, call time.sleep().

Use Selenium's WebDriverWait method to wait for certain components to load.

From selenium.webdriver.common.by import By.

Selenium.webdriver.support.ui   import WebDriverWait

From   selenium.webdriver.support   import expected_conditions as EC.

Example of waiting for an element to appear

element = WebDriverWait(driver, 10).until()

EC.presence_of_element_located(By.ID, 'element_id'))

Handling infinite scrolling:

To simulate scrolling, send JavaScript commands to the browser.

Scroll to the bottom of the page.

```
Driver.execute_script("window.scrollTo(0,
document.body.scrollHeight);"
```

```
time.sleep(5) # Wait for fresh content to load.
```

Dealing with pop-ups and modals:

Close pop-ups and modals by clicking their close buttons.

Close the modal or pop-up

```
Close_button                              =
driver.find_element(By.CLASS_NAME,     'close-
button-class').
```

```
close_button.click()
```

Selenium and Puppeteer are powerful tools that allow you to scrape data from modern web applications that use JavaScript to load content. These tools are capable of executing JavaScript and interacting with dynamic web pages.

Chapter 21

Advanced Methods for Dynamic Content Extraction

When working with complicated websites that mainly rely on JavaScript to load material dynamically, more advanced strategies are required. Here are some advanced techniques for extracting dynamic content using Selenium and other tools.

1. Handle JavaScript Execution

Waiting for Javascript to execute:

You can use JavaScript itself or wait for particular circumstances to confirm that JavaScript has finished executing and that the material has fully loaded.

Example:

From selenium.webdriver.common.by import By.

Selenium. web driver. support.ui import WebDriverWait

From selenium. webdriver. support import expected_conditions as EC.

```
# Wait till the element is present.

element = WebDriverWait(driver, 10).until()

EC.presence_of_element_located((By.ID,
'dynamic_element_id').)
```

Custom Javascript Execution:

Run custom JavaScript to guarantee that all data is loaded.

```
driver.execute_script("""

Return document.readyState === 'complete'.

""")
```

2. Interact with Elements

Filling up and submitting forms:

To scrape data that needs a form submission.

Example:

Find the form components and submit.

```
Search box = driver.find_element(By.NAME, 'q')

search_box.send_keys("example query")

search_box.submit()
```

Handling dropdowns and checkboxes:

```
from selenium.webdriver.support.UI import


# Choose an option from the dropdown

dropdown    =    Select(driver.find_element(By.ID,
'dropdown_id').

dropdown.select_by_visible_text("Option Text").


# Click a checkbox.

Checkbox        =        driver.find_element(By.ID,
'checkbox_id')

checkbox.click()
```

3. Managing pop-ups, alerts, and frames.

Closing Pop-ups:

Switch to the alert and accept it.

Alert = driver.switch_to.alert.

alert.accept()

Handling Frames:

To interact with components within frames.

Example:

Navigate to a frame by name or ID

driver.switch_to.frame('frame_name_or_id')

Go back to the default content

driver.switch_to.default_content()

4. Taking screenshots

Taking screenshots can be beneficial for troubleshooting and data collection.

Example:

Save a screenshot of the current page.

driver.save_screenshot('screenshot.png')

5. Scraping infinite scrolling pages.

Infinite scrolling sites load more material as you scroll down. Here's a reliable method:

Example:

Last_height = driver.execute_script("return document.body.scrollHeight").

While True:

Scroll to the bottom.

```
Driver.execute_script("window.scrollTo(0,
document.body.scrollHeight);"
```

time.sleep(5) Wait for fresh content to load.

Calculate the new scroll height and compare it to the previous height.

```
new_height    =    driver.execute_script("Return
document.body.scrollHeight").
```

If new_height equals last_height:

break

Last_height equals new_height

6. Extracting data from single-page applications.

SPAs dynamically refresh the page's content without requiring a full reload; use Selenium to interact with these pages in the same way a user would.

Example:

Click a button to load further material.

```
load_more_button                                    =
driver.find_element(By.ID,'load_more_button').

load_more_button.click()

time.sleep(5) # Wait for the content to load.
```

7. Using Headless Browsers.

Running browsers in headless mode (without a GUI) can help speed up the scraping process.

Headless mode in Chrome:

```
From selenium.webdriver.chrome.options import Options.

Options = Options().

options.add_argument("--headless")

Driver: webdriver.Chrome(options=options)
```

8. Using Proxies and User Agents.

To evade detection and blockage by websites, utilize proxies and change your user agent.

Setting Proxies:

from selenium. web driver.common.proxy import Proxy, ProxyType.

proxy = Proxy();

proxy.proxy_type is ProxyType.MANUAL.

proxy.http_proxy: 'http://your_proxy:port'

Proxy.ssl_proxy = 'http://your_proxy:port'

capabilities: web   driver.Desired capabilities.CHROME

proxy.add_to_capabilities(capabilities)

Driver   = webdriver.Chrome(desired_capabilities=capabiliti es).

Modifying user agents:

Options = Options().

```python
options.add_argument("user-agent=Mozilla/5.0
(Windows NT 10.0; Win64; x64)
AppleWebKit/537.36 (KHTML, like Gecko)
Chrome/91.0.4472.124 Safari/537.36")
```

Driver: webdriver.Chrome(options=options)

9. Capturing Network Traffic

To collect network data and analyze API calls, use browser developer tools such as Selenium Wire.

Selenium Wire:

```python
from SeleniumWire import webdriver
```

Driver = webdriver.Chrome().

```python
# Access requests via the driver.requests property.
driver.get('http://example.com')
```

for request in driver.requests.

If request.response:

print(request.url, response.status_code, headers)

10. Scraping data with Pyppeteer

Pyppeteer provides greater control over headless browsers.

Example:

```
import asyncio.

from Python, import launch

asynchronous def main():

Browser = await launch (headless=True)

page = await browser.newPage().

await page.goto('http://example.com').
```

```
await
page.waitForSelector('#dynamic_element_id').

content = await page.content().

await browser.close().

print(content)

asyncio.get_event_loop().run_until_complete(mai
n())
```

Advanced dynamic content extraction necessitates handling JavaScript execution, user interactions, infinite scrolling, and more. You can effectively scrape data from complex, modern web applications by using Selenium, Pyppeteer, and other techniques such as modifying user agents and capturing network traffic.

Chapter 22

Parsing the extracted data

After you've extracted HTML content with tools like Selenium or Pyppeteer, you'll need to parse it to get the information you need. Common methods for parsing HTML content include BeautifulSoup, LXML, and regular expressions (regex). Here's a step-by-step guide to effectively parsing extracted data.

1. Using BeautifulSoup.

Installation:

Copy code.

pip install beautifulsoup4 lxml.

Create a BeautifulSoup Object:

From bs4 import BeautifulSoup.

HTML_content = """"<!DOCTYPE HTML><html><head>

Title: Example
Page</head><body><h1>Heading</h1>

This is an opening paragraph.

<div id="content">.<p class="text">A paragraph within a div.</p><a href="http://example.com"class="link">

An example link</a>.</div></body></html>"""

soup = BeautifulSoup(html_content, 'lxml').

2. Finding the Elements

Find Elements by Tag Name:

```
h1_tag = soup.find("h1").

print(h1_tag.get_text())
```

Find All Elements by Tag Name:

```
p_tags = soup.find_all("p").

For p in p_tags:

print(p.get_text())
```

Finding Elements by Attribute:

```
intro_p = soup.find('p', class = 'intro')

print(intro_p.get_text())

Content_Div = soup.find('div', id='content')

print(content_div.get_text())
```

3. Applying CSS Selectors

CSS selectors are an effective approach to locating components in HTML.

Example:

```
Intro_p = soup.select_one('p.intro')

print(intro_p.get_text())

Links = soup.select('a.link')

For the link in links:

Print(link.get_text(), link['href'])
```

4. Navigating the HTML Tree

Parental and Sibling Navigation:

```
Parent_div = intro_p.find_parent('div').

print(parent_div)

Next_sibling = intro_p.find_next_sibling('p').

print(next_sibling.get_text())
```

Children and descendants:

```
Content_children = content_div.findChildren().

For the kid in content_children:

Print (child.name, child.get_text())

Content_descendants = content_div.find_all()

For descendant in content_descendants:

Print (descendant.name, descendant.get_text())
```

5. Extracting Data from Attributes.

Getting Attribute Values:

```
Link = soup.find('a', class_='link')

print(link['href'])
```

Handling Missing Attributes:

link_href = link.get('href', 'No href attribute').

print(link_href)

6. Parsing Tables.

Example:

HTML_Table
="""<table><tr><th>Name</th><th>Age</th></tr
><tr><td>Alice</td><td>30</td></tr><tr><td>Bob
</td><td>25</td></tr></table>"""

soup = BeautifulSoup(html_table, 'lxml').

Extract table headers.

Headers = [header.get_text() for header in
soup.find_all('th')].

print(headers)

Extract table rows.

```
rows = []

For each row in soup.find_all('tr')[1:]:

Columns = row.find_all('td').

rows.append([column.get_text() for column in
columns].

print(rows)
```

7. Using LXML.

Installation:

pip install lxml.

Parsing with LXML:

From lxml import html.

```
HTML_content = """

<!DOCTYPE HTML>

<html>

<head>
```

Title: Example Page

</head>

<body>

<h1>Heading</h1>

This is an opening paragraph.

<div id="content">.

<p class="text">A paragraph within a div.</p>

<a   href="http://example.com"   class="link">An example link</a>.

</div>

</body>

</html>
"""

Tree = HTML.fromstring(html_content)

Extracting elements.

```
h1_text = tree.xpath('//h1/text()', [0]

print(h1_text)


p_texts = tree.xpath('//p/text()').

For text in p_texts:

print(text)


# Extracting characteristics.

Links = tree.xpath('//a/@href').

For the link in links:

print(link)
```

8. Using Regular Expressions.

Regex may be used to extract certain patterns of data from HTML text.

Example:

```
Import re

HTML_content = """

<html>

<body>

This is an opening paragraph.

<p class="text">A paragraph within a div.</p>

</body>

</html>

"""

# Find all paragraph texts.

Paragraphs = re.find all(r'<p
class=".*?"'">(.*?)</p>" (html_content)

For p in paragraphs:

print(p)
```

Using tools like BeautifulSoup, lxml, and regular expressions, you can effectively navigate and extract the information you need from HTML content. Each tool has its own strengths, and selecting the right one depends on the complexity of the task and your specific needs. With these techniques, you can efficiently process and analyze data from multiple web sources.

Chapter 23

Handling Errors and Exceptions during Web Scraping

Errors and exceptions are frequently encountered in web scraping due to network issues, dynamic content, or changes in website structure. To ensure that your scraping scripts are robust and reliable, here's a detailed guide on how to handle them effectively.

1. Common Errors in Web Scraping

Network Errors:

Connection errors

Timeout errors

HTTP Error: 404 Not Found.

403. Forbidden 500. Internal Server Error.

Parsing errors include "Element not found."

Attribute not found.

Data handling errors include missing data and difficulties with data types.

2. Using Try-Except Blocks.

To gracefully handle exceptions, wrap potentially failing code in try-except blocks.

Example:

the code and test the following: response = requests.get('http://example.com') Response.raise_for_status() # Raises HTTPError for incorrect answers.

Content equals reaction. Content excludes requests. exceptions.Using RequestException as e, print "Request failed: {e}".

3. Handle Network and HTTP Errors

To handle network and HTTP problems, use the exception handling provided in the requests library.

Example:

Python: Copy code, and import requests.

url: 'http://example.com'

Try Response = Requests.Get(URL, timeout=10) Response.raise_for_status() # Raises HTTPError for faulty replies, except requests. exceptions.Timeout: print("The request timed out") except for requests. exceptions.TooManyRedirects: print("Too many redirects") except for requests. exceptions. Using RequestException as e, print "Request failed: {e}".

else: print("Request succeeded").

   # Process the material here.

4. Handling Parsing Errors Using BeautifulSoup

When processing HTML, items may not always appear. Handle these instances with try-except blocks or check for None.

Example:

Copy the code from bs4 and import BeautifulSoup.

HTML_content = """ <html>

<head> <title>Example Page: </title> </head> <body> <h1>Heading: </h1> </body> </html> ""

soup = BeautifulSoup(html_content, 'lxml').

Try this: Paragraph = soup.find('p')

   Print(paragraph.get_text())   except AttributeError: print("Paragraph not found").

Alternative with Conditionals:

paragraph = soup.find('p')

If paragraph

```
print(paragraph.get_text())
```

else: print("Paragraph not found").

5. Retry Requests

Implement retry logic to deal with temporary failures such as network outages or server overload.

Example Using Requests and Time:

Python steps include copying code, importing requests, and importing time.

url: 'http://example.com'

max_retries = five.

Retry_delay = 5.

For each attempt in the range (max_retries), try the following: response = requests.Get(url, timeout=10) Response.raise_for_status()

Break the loop if the request is successful (except   for requests).exceptions.RequestException as e.

print(f"Request failed (attempt {attempt + 1}): {e}")

If attempt < max_retries - 1: time.Sleep (retry_delay) Else:

print("Maximum retries exceeded")

6. Use Selenium for Robust Error Handling

Selenium scripts can fail for a variety of reasons, including items not found or timeouts. Use try-except blocks to handle these exceptions.

Example:

Copy code from Selenium. Import web driver from Selenium.   common.Exceptions.   Import

NoSuchElementException and TimeoutException from Selenium WebDriver Chrome Service. Service: selenium.webdriver.chrome.options import Options: from webdriver_manager.chrome import ChromeDriverManager.

Chrome_options = Options().

chrome_options.add_argument("--headless")

service = ChromeDriverManager().install())

Driver equals webdriver.Chrome(service = service; options = chrome_options)

Try this: driver. get('http://example.com').

element = driver.find_element_by_id('non_existent_id') except NoSuchElementException: print("Element not found") except TimeoutException: print("Loading timed out").

Finally, call the driver. quit().

7. Logging for Better Debugging.

Errors can be logged rather than printed to aid in debugging and log maintenance.

Example:

Python: Copy code, import logging.

```
# Set up logging setup.

Logging.basicConfig(filename='scraping.log',
level=logging).ERROR:
format='%(asctime)s:%(levelname)s:%(message)s'.
```

```
Try                  Response                =
Requests.get('http://example.com')
Response.raise_for_status() does not apply to
requests.exceptions.RequestException    as    e:
Logging.Error: "Request failed: {e}".
```

8. Validating Data: Ensure the extracted data satisfies anticipated formats and values.

Example:

data = soup.Find('p', class='intro').If get_text() does not return any data, logging will occur. Error: "No data found"

Elif is not data.isalpha() logs.Error: "Invalid data format: {data}".

Otherwise: print(data).

9. Graceful shutdown

Ensure that resources, such as browser instances, are correctly closed in the event of an error.

Example:

Try this: driver = webdriver.Chrome(service=service, options=chrome_options).

  driver.get('http://example.com')

  # Perform scraping procedures.

Finally, call the driver. quit().

Handling errors and exceptions is critical in web scraping to ensure that your scripts are durable and robust. Try-except blocks, retry logic, logging, and correct resource management may help you handle many sorts of problems and guarantee that your scraping processes execute smoothly. These strategies will assist you in developing more dependable web scrapers capable of handling unforeseen errors gracefully.

Chapter 24

Cleaning and preparing scraped data.

After extracting data from websites, it is typically untidy and has to be cleaned and prepared before it can be utilized efficiently for analysis or storage. Here's a full tutorial on how to clean and prepare scraped data in Python.

1. Common Data Cleaning Tasks.

Remove HTML Tags: Remove HTML tags from the text.

Missing Data Management: Fill in or eliminate any missing data.

Normalizing Data: Standardize forms (such as dates and currencies).

Removing Duplicates: Remove any duplicate entries.

Converting Data Types: Make that the data is in the right format (for example, converting strings to integers).

2. Remove HTML Tags

To clean text from HTML tags, use BeautifulSoup.

Example:

Copy the code from bs4 and import BeautifulSoup.

HTML_content: "<p>This is a bolded paragraph.</p>"Soup = BeautifulSoup(html_content, 'lxml')

Clean_text = soup.get_text(); print(clean_text). # Output: This is a bold paragraph.

3. Handling Missing Data.

Using Pandas to manage missing data in a DataFrame.

Example:

Python: Copy the code and import pandas as pd.

Example data = {'Name': ['Alice', 'Bob', None], 'Age': [30, None, 25]}.

df = pd.DataFrame(data)

To fill missing data with a placeholder, use df. fill ('Unknown', inplace=True) followed by print(df).

Remove rows with missing values: df.dropna(inplace=True) print(df)

4. Normalizing Data.

Standardizing data formats like dates and currencies.

Example:

from datetime and import it.

Date_str: "2024-06-11"

date_obj equals datetime.strptime(date_string, "%Y-%m-%d")

print(date_obj) # Output: 2024-06-11 00:00:00.

For currency normalization:

Import re.

Define normalize_currency(value): return float(re.sub(r'[^\d.]', '', value))

Currency_str: "$1,234.56"

normalized_value =
normalize_currency(currency_str)
print(normalized_value) Result: 1234.56

5. Remove Duplicates

Using Pandas to eliminate duplicates from a data frame.

Example:

Copy the code: data = {'Name': ['Alice', 'Bob', 'Alice'], 'Age': [30, 25, 30]}.

```
df = pd.DataFrame(data)
```

```
#                  Remove                  duplicates:
df.drop_duplicates(inplace=True).
```

```
print(df)
```

6. Converting data types

Ensure that data is in the proper format, such as converting strings to integers.

Example:

Copy the code: data = {'Name': ['Alice', 'Bob'], 'Age': ['30', '25']}.

```
df = pd.DataFrame(data).
```

```
# Convert Age to an integer.
```

```
df['Age']        equals        df['Age'].Astype(int)
Print(df.dtypes)
```

7. Handling whitespace and case

Trim whitespace and standardize text case.

Example:

Copy the code: text = "This is a sample text." cleaned_text = text.strip().Lower() Print(cleaned_text) # Here's a sample text for Pandas DataFrame:

Copy the code: data = {'Name': [' Alice ', 'Bob'], 'Occupation': [' Engineer ',' Developer']}.

df = pd.DataFrame(data)

Remove whitespace df = df.applymap(str.strip).

Standardize case.

df['Occupation'] equals df['Occupation'].Use str.lower() to print pdf.

8. Regular Cleaning Expressions

Regex is used to tidy up the more complicated language.

Example:

Import re.

text stands for "This is a sample text with numbers 1234 and special characters !@#."

clean_text = re.sub(r'[^A-Za-z\s]', '', text) print(cleaned_text) Output: Here is an example text containing numbers and special characters.

9. Parsing JSON data

If your data is in JSON format, use the JSON module to parse and clean it.

Example:

Import JSON

json_data = '{"name": "Alice", "age": 30}' parsed_data = json. loads(json_data).

Print the parsed data. Output: {'name':'Alice', 'age':30}

10. Saving Clean Data

Using Pandas to export cleaned data to CSV or Excel files.

Example:

```
df.to_csv('cleaned_data.csv',          index=False)
df.to_excel('cleaned_data.xlsx', index=False).
```

Example Workflow

Here's a whole sample workflow, from scraping to cleaning data:

Scraping:

Copy code from bs4 and import BeautifulSoup, then request.

url: 'http://example.com'

Response = requests.get(url).

soup = BeautifulSoup(response.content,'lxml')

Extract data Data = [] For each item in soup.find_all('div',   class='item'):   name   =

item.find('h2').get_text(strip=True);   age   = item.find('span', class = 'age').get_text(strip=True) returns data.append({'Name': name; 'Age': age})

Cleaning:

import pandas as pd, and then import re.

Convert to DataFrame: df = pd.DataFrame(data).

Remove the HTML tags (if any)

df['Name'] equals df['Name'].Apply(lambda x, BeautifulSoup(x, 'lxml').get_text())

Handle missing values: df['Age'].replae('', None, inplace=True)   df.dropna(subset=['Age'], inplace=True).

Convert Age to an integer df['Age'] = df['Age'].Apply(lambda x: int(re.sub(r'[^\d]', '', x))

Save   cleaned   data   with df.to_csv('cleaned_data.csv', index=False).

Cleaning and preparing scraped data is an important stage in the data extraction process.

You may rapidly clean and standardize your data using tools such as BeautifulSoup, Pandas, and regular expressions, ensuring that it is suitable for analysis and storage. Following these guidelines can help you deal with typical data challenges and preserve data quality.

1. Common Errors in Web Scraping

Network Errors:

Connection errors

Timeout errors

HTTP Error: 404 Not Found.

403. Forbidden 500. Internal Server Error.

Parsing errors include "Element not found."

Attribute not found.

Data handling errors include missing data and difficulties with data types.

2. Using Try-Except Blocks.

To gracefully handle exceptions, wrap potentially failing code in try-except blocks.

Example:

Copy the code and test the following: response = requests.get('http://example.com') Response.raise_for_status() # Raises HTTPError for incorrect answers.

Content equals reaction. Content excludes requests. exceptions.Using RequestException as e, print "Request failed: {e}".

3. Handle Network and HTTP Errors

To handle network and HTTP problems, use the exception handling provided in the requests library.

Example:

import requests.

url: 'http://example.com'

Try Response = Requests.Get(URL, timeout=10) Response.raise_for_status() # Raises HTTPError for faulty replies, except requests. exceptions.Timeout: print("The request timed out") except for requests. exceptions.TooManyRedirects: print("Too many redirects") except for requests. exceptions.Using RequestException as e, print "Request failed: {e}".

else: print("Request succeeded").

   # Process the material here.

4. Handling Parsing Errors Using BeautifulSoup

When processing HTML, items may not always appear. Handle these instances with try-except blocks or check for None.

Example:

Copy the code from bs4 and import BeautifulSoup.

HTML_content = """ <html>

<head> <title>Example Page: </title> </head> <body> <h1>Heading: </h1> </body> </html> ""

soup = BeautifulSoup(html_content, 'lxml').

Try this: Paragraph = soup.find('p')

Print(paragraph.get_text())   except AttributeError: print("Paragraph not found").

Alternative with Conditionals:

paragraph = soup.find('pm)

If paragraph

print(paragraph.get_text())

else: print("Paragraph not found").

5. Retry Requests

Implement retry logic to deal with temporary failures such as network outages or server overload.

Example Using Requests and Time:

Python steps include copying code, importing requests, and importing time.

url: 'http://example.com'

max_retries = five.

Retry_delay = 5.

For each attempt in the range (max_retries), try the following: response = requests.Get(url, timeout=10) Response.raise_for_status()

Break the loop if the request is successful (except   for requests).exceptions.RequestException as e.

print(f"Request failed (attempt {attempt + 1}): {e}")

If attempt < max_retries - 1: time.Sleep (retry_delay) Else:

```
print("Maximum retries exceeded")
```

6. Use Selenium for Robust Error Handling

Selenium scripts can fail for a variety of reasons, including items not found or timeouts. Use try-except blocks to handle these exceptions.

Example:

Copy code from Selenium. Import web driver from Selenium. common.Exceptions. Import NoSuchElementException and TimeoutException from Selenium WebDriver Chrome Service. Service: selenium.webdriver.chrome.options import Options: from webdriver_manager.chrome import ChromeDriverManager.

```
Chrome_options = Options().
```

```
chrome_options.add_argument("--headless")
```

```
service = ChromeDriverManager().install())
```

Driver equals webdriver.Chrome(service = service; options = chrome_options)

Try this: driver. get('http://example.com').

```
    element                                  =
driver.find_element_by_id('non_existent_id')
except NoSuchElementException: print("Element
not found") except TimeoutException:
print("Loading timed out").
```

Finally, call the driver. quit().

7. Logging for Better Debugging.

Errors can be logged rather than printed to aid in debugging and log maintenance.

Example

Python: Copy code, import logging.

Set up logging setup.

Logging.basicConfig(filename='scraping.log', level=logging).ERROR: format='%(asctime)s:%(levelname)s:%(message)s'.

Try Response = Requests.get('http://example.com') Response.raise_for_status() does not apply to requests.exceptions.RequestException as e: Logging.Error: "Request failed: {e}".

8. Validating Data: Ensure the extracted data satisfies anticipated formats and values.

Example:

data = soup.Find('p', class='intro').If get_text() does not return any data, logging will occur. Error: "No data found"

Elif is not data.isalpha() logs.Error: "Invalid data format: {data}".

Otherwise: print(data).

9. Graceful shutdown

Ensure that resources, such as browser instances, are correctly closed in the event of an error.

Example:

Try this: driver = webdriver.Chrome(service=service, options=chrome_options).

```
driver.get('http://example.com')

# Perform scraping procedures.
```

Finally, call the driver. quit().

Handling errors and exceptions are critical in web scraping to ensure that your scripts are durable and robust. Try-except blocks, retry logic, logging, and correct resource management may help you handle many sorts of problems and guarantee that your scraping processes execute smoothly. These strategies will assist you in developing more dependable web scrapers capable of handling unforeseen errors gracefully.

Chapter 25

Cleaning and preparing scraped data.

After extracting data from websites, it is typically untidy and has to be cleaned and prepared before it can be utilized efficiently for analysis or storage. Here's a full tutorial on how to clean and prepare scraped data in Python.

1. Common Data Cleaning Tasks.

Remove HTML Tags: Remove HTML tags from the text.

Missing Data Management: Fill in or eliminate any missing data.

Normalizing Data: Standardize forms (such as dates and currencies).

Removing Duplicates: Remove any duplicate entries.

Converting Data Types: Make that the data is in the right format (for example, converting strings to integers).

2. Remove HTML Tags

To clean text from HTML tags, use BeautifulSoup.

Example:

from bs4 and import BeautifulSoup.

HTML_content: "<p>This is a bolded paragraph.</p>"Soup = BeautifulSoup(html_content, 'lxml')

Clean_text = soup.get_text(); print(clean_text). # Output: This is a bold paragraph.

3. Handling Missing Data.

Using Pandas to manage missing data in a DataFrame.

Example:

Python: Copy the code and import pandas as pd.

```python
# Example data = {'Name': ['Alice', 'Bob', None],
'Age': [30, None, 25]}.

df = pd.DataFrame(data)
```

To fill missing data with a placeholder, use df. fill ('Unknown', inplace=True) followed by print(df).

```python
# Remove rows with missing values:
df.dropna(inplace=True) print(df)
```

4. Normalizing Data.

Standardizing data formats like dates and currencies.

Example:

from datetime and import it.

Date_str: "2024-06-11"

date_obj equals datetime.strptime(date_string, "%Y-%m-%d")

print(date_obj) Output: 2024-06-11 00:00:00.

For currency normalization:

Import re.

Define normalize_currency(value): return float(re.sub(r'[^\d.]', '', value))

Currency_str: "$1,234.56"

normalized_value = normalize_currency(currency_str) print(normalized_value) Result: 1234.56

5. Remove Duplicates

Using Pandas to eliminate duplicates from a data frame.

Example:

data = {'Name': ['Alice', 'Bob', 'Alice'], 'Age': [30, 25, 30]}.

df = pd.DataFrame(data)

Remove   duplicates:
df.drop_duplicates(inplace=True).

print(df)

6. Converting data types

Ensure that data is in the proper format, such as converting strings to integers.

Example:

data = {'Name': ['Alice', 'Bob'], 'Age': ['30', '25']}.

df = pd.DataFrame(data).

Convert Age to an integer.

df['Age']   equals   df['Age'].Astype(int)
Print(df.dtypes)

7. Handling whitespace and case

Trim whitespace and standardize text case.

Example:

text = "This is a sample text." cleaned_text = text. strip().Lower() Print(cleaned_text) # Here's a sample text for Pandas DataFrame:

data = {'Name': [' Alice ', 'Bob'], 'Occupation': [' Engineer ',' Developer']}.

df = pd.DataFrame(data)

Remove whitespace df = df. applymap(str. strip).

Standardize case.

df['Occupation'] equals df['Occupation'].Use str.lower() to print

8. Regular Cleaning Expressions

Regex is used to tidy up the more complicated language.

Example:

Python: Copy code Import re.

the text stands for "This is a sample text with numbers 1234 and special characters !@#."

```python
clean_text = re.sub(r'[^A-Za-z\s]', '', text)
```
print(cleaned_text) Output: Here is an example text containing numbers and special characters.

9. Parsing JSON data

If your data is in JSON format, use the JSON module to parse and clean it.

Example:

Python: Copy code Import JSON

```python
json_data = '{"name": "Alice", "age": 30}'
parsed_data = json. loads(json_data).
```

Print the parsed data. Output: {'name':'Alice', 'age':30}

10. Saving Clean Data

Using Pandas to export cleaned data to CSV or Excel files.

Example:

```
df.to_csv('cleaned_data.csv',          index=False)
df.to_excel('cleaned_data.xlsx', index=False).
```

Example Workflow

Here's a whole sample workflow, from scraping to cleaning data:

Scraping:

from bs4 and import BeautifulSoup, then request.

url: 'http://example.com'

Response = requests.get(url).

soup = BeautifulSoup(response.content,'lxml')

Extract data Data = [] For each item in soup.find_all('div', class='item'): name = item.find('h2').get_text(strip=True); age = item.find('span', class = 'age').get_text(strip=True) returns data.append({'Name': name; 'Age': age})

Cleaning:

import pandas as pd, and then import re.

Convert to DataFrame: df = pd.DataFrame(data).

Remove the HTML tags (if any)

df['Name'] equals df['Name'].Apply(lambda x, BeautifulSoup(x, 'lxml').get_text())

Handle missing values: df['Age'].replace('', None, inplace=True) df.dropna(subset=['Age'], inplace=True).

Convert Age to an integer df['Age'] = df['Age'].Apply(lambda x: int(re.sub(r'[^\d]', '', x))

Save cleaned data with df.to_csv('cleaned_data.csv', index=False).

Cleaning and preparing scraped data is an important stage in the data extraction process. You may rapidly clean and standardize your data using tools such as BeautifulSoup, Pandas, and regular expressions, ensuring that it is suitable for analysis and storage. Following these guidelines can help you deal with typical data challenges and preserve data quality.

1. Proxy Rotation.

Proxy rotation is the process of moving between different proxies in order to circumvent detection and IP-based limitations. There are numerous methods for implementing proxy rotation:

a. Utilize Proxy Pools: Create a collection of proxies from many providers or sources.

For each request, rotate through the pool's proxies.

b. Rotate Proxies Automatically: Set up logic to rotate proxies after a particular number of requests or time period.

Monitor proxy performance and rotate according to availability and response times.

c. Dynamic Proxy Acquisition: Use services or libraries for dynamic proxy acquisition.

Always fetch and utilize new proxies from these providers.

2. IP Blocking Prevention.

Preventing IP blocking entails using tactics to prevent detection and reduce the chance of being banned by websites.

a. Simulate human behavior by inserting pauses between queries.

Randomize user-agent strings so that they seem like distinct web browsers or devices.

To replicate real-world user interaction, emulate mouse movements, scrolling, and clicking.

b. Use Proxies for Residential IPs: Residential IPs are less likely to be banned than data center IPs.

Use proxies with residential IP addresses to prevent detection.

d. Rotate user sessions.

Maintained numerous user sessions by handling cookies and requests.

Rotate user sessions to mimic many users visiting the webpage.

d. Track Response Codes and Patterns:

Check response codes for indicators of IP blocking (e.g., frequent 403 Forbidden or 429 Too Many Requests messages).

Implement logic to identify and respond to IP blocking dynamically (for example, switching proxies or adjusting scraping pace).

f. Respect Robots.txt.

To understand scraping rules and constraints, refer to the website's robots.txt file.

Respect the robots.txt guidelines to avoid IP banning.

3. Error Handling and Logging.

Implement comprehensive error handling and logging tools to monitor scraping activity and identify problems.

Log proxy use, response codes, and any IP blocking events for future analysis and troubleshooting.

Proxy rotation and IP blocking avoidance are critical approaches for successful and sustained web scraping. By rotating proxies, simulating human activity, employing residential IP addresses, and analyzing response patterns, you may reduce the danger of IP blocking while ensuring ongoing and dependable scraping activities. Furthermore, strong error handling and recording tools are required for quickly recognizing and addressing difficulties.

How to handle captchas. CAPTCHAs (Completely Automated Public Turing Test to Tell Computers and Humans Apart) are a typical obstacle in web scraping since they are intended to restrict automated access to websites. Here are several techniques for handling CAPTCHAs:

1. Avoidance Techniques

To bypass known CAPTCHA pages, check if the website uses a certain URL pattern for CAPTCHA challenges.

Implement logic to detect and prevent scraping these pages in order to reduce encounters with CAPTCHAs.

b. Use alternate Data Sources: Look for alternate sources or APIs that offer comparable data without CAPTCHA issues.

Investigate paid data providers or APIs that enable access to structured data without CAPTCHAs.

2. CAPTCHA Solving Services.

a. Manual CAPTCHA Solving: Use human operators or services to manually solve CAPTCHAs.

Redirect CAPTCHA difficulties to humans for manual assistance.

b. Automated CAPTCHA Solving Services: Use third-party services using automated algorithms to solve CAPTCHAs.

Integrate APIs or libraries from CAPTCHA solution services into your scraping operation.

3. Machine Learning & OCR

Train machine learning models to automatically detect and solve CAPTCHAs.

CAPTCHA pictures may be analyzed and interpreted using image processing methods and convolutional neural networks.

b. Use optical character recognition (OCR) methods to retrieve text from CAPTCHA pictures.

Use libraries like Tesseract to recognize text from CAPTCHA pictures.

4. CAPTCHA Mitigation.

a. Delayed Scraping: Delay queries to emulate human behavior and decrease CAPTCHA encounters.

To avoid alerting CAPTCHA detection technologies, spread scraping jobs out over longer periods of time.

b. CAPTCHA Solving Threshold: Set a limit on the number of CAPTCHAs seen before taking action (e.g., switching proxies or employing CAPTCHA-solving services).

Implement logic that adjusts scraping activity based on the number of CAPTCHA challenges.

5. Legal and ethical considerations.

a. Follow the Website Terms of Service:

Adhere to the website's terms of service and scraping rules, which may ban you from evading CAPTCHAs or scraping protected material.

b. Use CAPTCHA solution Responsibly: To avoid detection and legal implications, avoid overusing CAPTCHA solution services.

CAPTCHAs must be handled in web scraping using a combination of avoidance tactics, CAPTCHA solution services, machine learning, OCR, and CAPTCHA mitigation measures. To prevent potential implications, CAPTCHA handling should be approached with prudence and in accordance with legal and ethical concerns. By using the correct strategies, you may efficiently manage CAPTCHA difficulties while scraping data from websites without interruption.

Chapter 26

User Agent Rotation

User-Agent rotation is a frequent approach in online scraping that simulates multiple browsers and devices, lowering the probability of being recognized and blacklisted by websites. Here's how to do user agent rotation:

1. User Agent Lists.

a. Generate a list of user-agent strings for various browsers, devices, and operating systems.

Include common user agents for desktop browsers (e.g., Chrome, Firefox, Safari) as well as mobile devices.

b. Rotate User-Agents: For each scrape request, choose a random user-agent from the list.

Implement logic to rotate user agents at regular intervals or after a given amount of queries.

2. User Agent Spoofing Libraries

a. Use Libraries for User-Agent Spoofing: Utilize libraries or frameworks with built-in spoofing capabilities.

Python libraries, such as fake-user agents, produce random user-agent strings for each request.

3. Custom User Agent Headers

a. Manually set user-agent headers for scraping requests.

Include a wide range of user-agent strings to emulate different browsers and devices.

4. Dynamic User Agent Generation

a. Generate user agents. Dynamically construct user-agent strings based on certain parameters, such as browser type, version, and platform.

Use libraries or methods to produce user-agent strings for each request as they occur.

5. User Agent Rotation Strategies

a. Random Rotation: Choose a random user-agent from the list for each request to prevent the discovery of trends.

To replicate organic traffic, provide a fair distribution of user agents.

b. Rotate user agents consecutively for each request.

When you get to the conclusion of the list, use logic to return to the beginning.

6. Monitoring and Adjustments.

a. Evaluate the efficacy of User-Agent rotation by monitoring website replies and blocking events.

Analyze reaction patterns and change rotation tactics as necessary to reduce detection.

User-agent rotation is a crucial approach for online scraping that allows you to imitate multiple browsers and devices while avoiding detection by websites. Rotating user-agent strings allows you to replicate organic traffic while reducing the chance of being blacklisted or tagged as a bot. To enable successful and long-term web scraping activities, a list of user agents must be created, rotation tactics selected, and efficacy monitored.

Chapter 27

Parallel scraping techniques

Parallel scraping approaches to speed up data extraction by dividing scraping jobs over numerous processes or threads. Here are several approaches for implementing simultaneous scraping:

1. Multi-threading

a. Thread Pooling: Set up a pool of worker threads to tackle scraping jobs.

Distribute URLs or tasks to many threads for concurrent execution.

b. Use asynchronous I/O libraries (e.g., asyncio) for non-blocking operations.

Execute scraping operations in parallel inside a single event loop.

2) Multiprocessing

a. Process Pooling: Set up a pool of worker processes to handle scraping jobs.

Use a task queue or a shared data structure to distribute tasks among processes.

b. Parallel Processing: Divide the scraping task into smaller bits and allocate each to a different process.

To obtain the final product, aggregate the results of various procedures.

3. Distributed Scraping a. Distributed Task Queues: Use Celery to divide scraping jobs across several workers.

Scale horizontally by hiring more people to meet the increased workload.

b. Message Passing: Use message brokers such as RabbitMQ or Kafka to distribute scraping jobs over different nodes.

Coordinate data retrieval and aggregation among dispersed nodes.

4. Asynchronous Scraping Libraries

a. Scrapy with Twisted: Combine the Scrapy framework with Twisted for asynchronous web scraping.

Scrapy includes built-in support for parallelism and distributed crawling.

b. Use asynchronous scraping libraries like aiohttp, requests-async, or httpx to handle concurrent HTTP queries.

To improve performance, perform scraping activities asynchronously. Additionally, load balancing is recommended.

a. Proxy Rotation: Rotate proxies or IP addresses to equally distribute scrape requests among servers or IP ranges.

Avoid overloading specific servers and minimize the possibility of IP banning.

b. Use load balancing to equally divide scraping work across different servers or instances. To improve performance, make sure that each server or instance handles a proportionate workload.

Parallel scraping approaches enable quicker and more effective data extraction by dividing scraping jobs over numerous processes, threads, or nodes. Parallel scraping, whether utilizing multithreading, multiprocessing, distributed scraping, or asynchronous libraries, increases the performance and scalability of large-scale scraping jobs. Load balancing and proxy rotation techniques also assist to spread workload equitably while avoiding discovery or IP blocking.

To maximize performance and reliability, select the best parallel scraping technique depending on your individual requirements and infrastructure limits.

Chapter 28

Load balancing and scaling

Load balancing and scalability are important factors when creating a web scraping system to achieve peak performance, dependability, and efficiency. Here's how to use load balancing and scalability in your web scraping infrastructure:

1. Load Balancing Techniques.

a. Round Robin: Distribute scrape requests evenly among numerous servers or instances in a circular pattern.

Each server handles the following request sequentially, guaranteeing a balanced burden distribution.

b. Least Connection: Send inbound requests to the server with the fewest active connections.

Ensure that servers with lighter loads receive more requests, resulting in balanced resource use.

c. Weighted Round Robin: Assign weights to scrape servers based on their capacity and performance.

Servers with higher weights receive a bigger proportion of inbound requests.

d. IP Hash: Use the client's IP address to generate a hash value and route the request to the appropriate server.

Ensure that requests from the same client are constantly directed to the same server, thereby preserving session affinity.

2. Scalability Strategies.

a. Horizontal Scaling: Add more scraping servers or instances to meet higher workloads or traffic.

Use load balancing techniques to uniformly distribute incoming requests among all servers.

Vertical scaling involves upgrading individual scraping servers or instances with more CPU, memory, or network capacity to accommodate rising workloads.

Monitor resource use and scale up servers as needed to ensure performance.

c. Auto-Scaling: Use auto-scaling strategies to add or remove scraping servers based on predetermined parameters like CPU utilization or request rate.

Ensure that the scraping infrastructure responds dynamically to changing workload circumstances.

d. Distributed Architecture: Create a scraping architecture that distributes jobs over numerous nodes or clusters.

Scraping jobs and aggregation results can be coordinated via distributed task queues or message-passing systems.

3. Monitoring and alerting

a. Performance Monitoring: Assess scraping infrastructure health and performance by monitoring important parameters including response time, throughput, and error rate.

Use monitoring tools and dashboards to display and evaluate performance indicators in real-time.

b. Resource utilization:

Monitor CPU, memory, disk, and network usage on scraping servers to discover possible bottlenecks or resource limits.

Scale resources horizontally or vertically to maximize resource consumption and performance.

c. Set alerts and notifications for key events including server failures, high error rates, and resource depletion.

Implement automatic response systems to quickly resolve issues and reduce downtime.

Load balancing and scalability are critical components of a strong web scraping architecture, as they provide effective resource use, high availability, and consistent performance. Scraping requests can be uniformly distributed over various servers or instances by using load balancing techniques like round robin, least connection, and weighted round robin.

Furthermore, scalability solutions like horizontal scaling, vertical scaling, auto-scaling, and distributed architecture allow your scraping infrastructure to adapt to changing workload circumstances and manage additional traffic efficiently. Monitoring resource use and performance indicators, as well as proactive alerts and automatic reaction mechanisms, all contribute to the scraping infrastructure's long-term health and stability.

Chapter 29

Optimization Tips for Efficient Scraping

Optimizing your web scraping process is critical for increasing efficiency, minimizing resource usage, and maintaining consistent performance. Here are some optimization techniques for effective web scraping:

1. Targeted Data Extraction.

a. Specify Target URLs: Extract data from relevant pages or URLs to reduce needless queries.

Use targeted URL patterns or filters to find particular sites that contain the needed data.

b. Selective Element Extraction: Identify and extract just necessary data items for your application.

Scraping whole web pages is unnecessary if just specified portions or properties are required.

2. Throttling and rate-limiting

a. Implement Delays: Delay scraping requests to avoid overwhelming target websites and decrease IP blocking risk.

Adjust delay times dependent on the website's responsiveness and scraping frequency.

b. Respect Robots.txt.

To understand scraping guidelines, refer to the target website's robots.txt file and follow any crawl-delay directives supplied.

Maintain a reasonable scraping pace by following crawl-delay suggestions.

3. Efficient network requests.

a. Use Persistent Connections: Use HTTP keep-alive connections to reuse TCP connections and minimize costs.

Maintain persistent connections for many queries to the same server to increase efficiency.

b. Use HTTP/2 protocol for better multiplexing, header compression, and efficient processing of simultaneous requests.

4. Proxy Management.

a. Rotate Proxies: Use a pool of proxies to disperse scraping requests and prevent IP blocking.

Monitor proxy performance and dynamically swap between proxies based on availability and dependability.

a. Use Proxy Pools: Use proxy pools supplied by third-party services or libraries to access a wide range of IP addresses without discovery.

5. HTML parsing

a. Use Efficient Parsing Libraries: Use lightweight HTML parsing libraries like BeautifulSoup or lxml for quicker performance.

Optimize the parsing code to reduce resource use and increase overall efficiency.

b. Minimize parsing overhead by extracting just necessary HTML elements or attributes.

Use selective parsing techniques to zero in on certain data pieces of interest.

6. Error-handling and retry mechanisms

Implement retry logic to appropriately handle temporary problems like connection timeouts and server faults.

Retry unsuccessful requests using exponential backoff tactics to prevent overloading the target servers.

b. Monitor and log scraping errors and exceptions.

Monitor error rates and change scraping behavior or retry settings as appropriate to reduce mistakes.

7. Scraping Policy Compliance

a. Respect Website conditions of Service: Follow scraping rules and conditions to preserve strong relationships with website owners.

Avoid aggressive scraping practices, which may breach website conditions and raise legal or ethical concerns.

b. Follow Scraping Etiquette: Identify yourself as a scraper by using suitable user-agent headers and according to scraping etiquette requirements.

Limit scraping frequency and volume to prevent interrupting website operations and affecting user experience.

You may maximize the efficiency and dependability of your online scraping process by using focused data extraction strategies, throttle and rate restriction, efficient network requests, proxy management, HTML parser optimization, error handling, and scraping policy compliance. Optimization tactics should promote courteous and responsible scraping activities in order to preserve positive relationships with target websites and ensure long-term scraping operations.

Chapter 30

Scraping data from e-commerce sites

Scraping data from e-commerce websites may give useful insights into competition analysis, price intelligence, product research, and market trends. Here's a general method for scraping data from e-commerce websites:

1. Identify target websites.

a. Choose E-commerce Platforms: Find websites related to your sector or target market.

Concentrate on prominent platforms like Amazon, eBay, Walmart, and Shopify shops.

b. Legal and ethical considerations: Review target websites' terms of service, scraping policies, and robots.txt files.

Maintain compliance with website scraping rules and refrain from breaking website conditions.

2. Define Scraping Scope a. Determine Data Requirements: Identify the precise categories of data to scrape, such as product details, pricing, reviews, ratings, and more.

Define the desired output data's structure and format (for example, CSV, JSON, database).

b. Choose categories or products:

Choose product categories, brands, or particular goods to scrape based on your study objectives.

Focus on high-value or trending goods to gain useful insights.

3. Develop a Scraping Strategy.

a. Choose Scraping Tools and Libraries: Choose web scraping tools and libraries based on your programming language (e.g., Python, JavaScript).

Popular possibilities include BeautifulSoup, Scrapy, Selenium, Puppeteer, and others.

b. Apply Data Extraction Logic:

Create scraping code to explore target e-commerce websites, identify important parts, and collect the needed data.

To locate and extract data, use CSS selectors, XPath expressions, or DOM traversal techniques.

4. Manage Pagination and Dynamic Content.

a. Pagination Handling: Add logic to traverse across several pages of product listings.

Extract data from each page and combine the results for a thorough study.

b. Dynamic Content Management:

Use dynamic scraping tools (e.g., Selenium, Puppeteer) to interact with JavaScript or AJAX-loaded items.

Make sure that all essential data is recorded, including dynamically loaded material like reviews or product variations.

5. Implement error-handling and retry mechanisms.

a. Handle HTTP Errors: Add logic to gracefully handle HTTP errors (e.g., 404, 503).

Retry unsuccessful requests using exponential backoff algorithms to reduce interruptions.

c. Monitor and log errors:

Implement logging methods to track scraping problems and exceptions.

Log error information for troubleshooting and debugging reasons.

6. Follow Website Policies and Limits

a. Implement rate restriction and throttling to manage scrape frequency and prevent IP blocking.

Respect website scraping policies and avoid using aggressive scraping strategies.

b. Use randomized user agents and proxies to simulate human activity and prevent discovery.

Use proxy rotation methods to disperse scraping requests while minimizing the impact on target websites.

7. Test and validate scraping results.

a. Test Scenarios: Extensively test your scraping code in many scenarios and edge cases.

Validate scraped data against recognized sources or do manual checks to ensure its accuracy and completeness.

b. Handle Edge Cases: Address issues like missing data, unusual formats, or changes in website layout.

Implement strong error handling and fallback techniques to handle edge circumstances appropriately.

Scraping data from e-commerce websites necessitates meticulous organization, execution, and respect for legal and ethical standards. You can extract valuable data for analysis and insights by taking a systematic approach to identify target websites, defining scraping scope, developing scraping strategies, dealing with pagination and dynamic content, implementing error handling and retry mechanisms, respecting website policies and limits, and testing and validating scraping results.

Chapter 31

Extracting Data from Social Media Platforms

Extracting data from social media networks may give useful insights for market research, sentiment analysis, trend tracking, and consumer feedback analysis. Here's a general method for obtaining data from social media platforms:

1. Select Social Media Platforms.

a. Choose appropriate social media channels for your sector, target audience, and study aims.

Consider prominent networks like Twitter, Facebook, Instagram, LinkedIn, and Reddit.

b. Evaluate Platform APIs and Data Availability: Consider the APIs and data access policies of potential social media platforms.

Determine the availability of public data, as well as any access limitations and rate limits.

2. Define data requirements.

a. Identify Data Sources: Determine the data types to extract, such as posts, comments, likes, shares, and hashtags.

Define the scope and duration for data collection (e.g., past week, past month).

b. Specify relevant search queries, hashtags, or keywords for your study aims.

Advanced search operators are useful for narrowing down search results and filtering relevant material.

3. Select Scraping Tools and APIs.

a. Use official APIs from social media networks to obtain public data.

Register for API access, acquire authentication credentials, and follow the API usage instructions.

b. Utilize Third-Party Libraries and Tools: Research third-party libraries and tools that offer wrappers or SDKs for social media APIs.

Popular libraries include Tweepy (Twitter), Facebook Graph API SDK, Instagram API Python SDK, PRAW (Reddit API), and so on.

4. Develop Scraping Logic.

To connect to social media APIs, use OAuth tokens or API keys for authentication.

To access data endpoints, establish connections, and authenticate requests. Then, implement extraction logic by writing code to get data based on search queries, hashtags, and user profiles.

Extract useful metadata, content, and engagement analytics from social media postings and comments.

5. Manage pagination and rate limits.

a. Pagination Handling: Process paginated replies by iterating across several pages of search results or data endpoints.

Create logic to browse through pagination links, or use cursor-based pagination approaches.

b. Rate Limiting and Throttling: Use API rate limitations and throttling methods to manage request frequency.

Monitor API use limitations and modify scraping rates to prevent exceeding them.

6. Analyze and filter data.

a. Filter Relevant material: Use filters and criteria to extract relevant material from scraped data.

Remove duplicates, spam, and irrelevant posts to focus on high-quality information.

b. Optional: Perform sentiment analysis using natural language processing (NLP) on text data.

Examine the mood, thoughts, and emotions represented in social media postings and comments.

7. Store and analyze data.

a. Choose Data Storage Solutions: Consider databases (e.g., SQL, NoSQL), data lakes, or cloud storage.

Create data schemas and frameworks for organizing and storing retrieved social media data efficiently.

b. Use data analysis and visualization tools to understand gathered social media data.

Develop insights, trends, and visualizations to aid decision-making and research goals.

To extract information from social media networks, a systematic strategy is required to access APIs, establish data needs, implement scraping logic, deal with pagination and rate constraints, evaluate and filter data, and properly

store and analyze data. You may use official APIs, third-party libraries, and scraping tools to access public data from social media networks and extract important insights for market research, sentiment analysis, and trend tracking. To guarantee ethical and responsible data scraping methods, follow API usage rules, observe rate restrictions, and adhere to platform standards.

Chapter 32

Real-world examples and challenges.

Real-world instances of scraping data from social networking networks are:

Twitter Sentiment Analysis: Scraping tweets about a given topic or hashtag and assessing sentiment to determine public opinion or trends.

Instagram Influencer Analysis: Using data from Instagram profiles and posts to identify influencers, assess engagement metrics, and evaluate influencer marketing campaigns.

Facebook Page Analytics includes scraping data from Facebook pages to measure likes, comments, shares, and other engagement indicators for performance analysis.

Reddit Trend Monitoring: Extracting posts and comments from Reddit communities to track discussions, analyze trends, and solicit user input.

LinkedIn Talent Acquisition: Scraping LinkedIn profiles to collect information about job searchers, assess their abilities and experience, and discover viable prospects for recruitment.

Scraping data from social media networks has several challenges, including:

API Limitations: Social media sites frequently put rate limitations, access restrictions, and data usage regulations on their APIs, which limit the quantity and frequency of data that may be scraped.

Data Privacy: Scraping user-generated material from social media sites presents privacy issues since it entails accessing and processing personal information. Compliance with data protection requirements, such as GDPR, is critical.

Dynamic Content: Social media networks often alter their user interfaces and offer dynamic content-loading systems, making it difficult to scrape data consistently. To deal with dynamic material, techniques like headless browsers and reverse engineering APIs may be required.

IP Blocking and Detection: Social media networks use anti-scraping mechanisms to identify and prevent scraping activities. IP rotation, user-agent rotation, and proxy management are all important techniques for avoiding discovery and blocking IP addresses.

Data Quality and Noise: Social media data frequently contains noise, spam, and irrelevant information, which can degrade the accuracy and dependability of analytic findings. Implementing data filtering and quality control techniques is critical for ensuring the accuracy of insights obtained from scraped data.

Ethical Considerations: Scraping data from social media networks poses issues of user permission, data ownership, and responsible scraping. Adhering to platform terms of service, respecting user privacy choices, and gaining consent when needed are all essential ethical issues.

Chapter 33

Conclusion

Web scraping has become a vital skill for data lovers, academics, and professionals from a variety of sectors. Throughout this book, we've looked at the fundamental concepts, ethical issues, and practical procedures required for successful web scraping. Understanding web page structure, using tools like BeautifulSoup and Selenium, and adopting advanced techniques like proxy rotation and parallel scraping will provide you with a full arsenal for extracting useful data swiftly and legally.

As you begin your online scraping journey, keep in mind the necessity of adhering to legal guidelines and website terms of service. Ethical scraping not only assures compliance but also promotes ethical data extraction practices. The case studies and real-world examples in this book should act as a guide and inspiration as you embark on your web scraping initiatives.

The area of online scraping is constantly changing, with new difficulties and possibilities emerging as the web expands. Stay curious, experiment, and learn to improve your talents and adapt to the changing world.

Thank you for joining me on this adventure. Happy scrapping!